Praise for *My Best Fi*

D0376942

"With the Pacific Ocean as his backdrop, Roger Thompson paints a firsthand picture of the reality that life is not easy. It's cruel, challenging, and hopeless; and being a Christian doesn't make it easy. He questions God's authority in the face of loss and rejection and draws closer to his Heavenly Father in the process. God has taken him on an incredible journey; one that we can all learn something from."

—JOSH TURNER, MULTI-PLATINUM
MCA NASHVILLE RECORDING ARTIST

"Life doesn't always turn out like we expect, and we must learn to celebrate every gift and mourn every loss. *My Best Friend's Funeral* will teach you to do both with resolve and grace."

—MARGARET FEINBERG, AUTHOR OF *Fight with Joy*

"A remarkable true story of a deep and true friendship. It's an emotional journey through joy, sorrow, and hope. With insight into living and loving more fully, my friend Roger shows us how to find meaning in the hardships we can't explain, and how love can grow from our deepest loss. Brutally honest and beautifully compassionate, it will inspire you to, once again, tell your family and friends how much you love them. You'll love reading this book."

—MICHAEL W. SMITH, SINGER-SONGWRITER

"Roger has been a close friend of mine for more than a decade. But in some ways this book introduced me to him for the first time. His writing displays incredible insights into life and loss that cut to the heart and will inspire you. His candor, warmth, and hope encourage us to become better fathers and mothers—and friends. I think you'll love this book."

—DAVID KINNAMAN, AUTHOR OF *unChristian* AND *You Lost Me*

"A profoundly moving, heartbreaking, and surprisingly hilarious story of an extraordinary friendship. Roger takes us to almost unbearable depths of grief and then through laughter and tears leaves us with the assurance that even our greatest suffering can turn to joy. It is a must read."

—MIKE FOSTER, AUTHOR; FOUNDER OF
PEOPLE OF THE SECOND CHANCE

"With raw honesty Roger Thompson invites us into his narrative of abandonment, friendship, and redemption. Thompson gives a poignant reminder that our stories shape us, and at the center of every story is the need for relationship."

—Pastor Chris Seay

"A gutsy and transparent memoir about the most important and difficult issues we face in this lifetime. It's a true story well told of friendship and fatherhood, love lost and found, grief, forgiveness, and ultimately, redemption. It speaks to me as a father and a man—and inspires me to be better at both."

—Mark Stuart, lead singer of Audio Adrenaline
and cofounder of The Hands and Feet Project

"A beautiful, poignant memoir of loss and life. *My Best Friend's Funeral* is a rare gift that will bring comfort, hope, and even companionship to those navigating the valley of the shadow whilst aspiring to the heights of a life well-lived."

—Pete Greig, author of *God on Mute: Engaging the Silence of Unanswered Prayer*

"Everybody has a secret fishing hole they are looking for. A place where everything makes sense and puts one at ease. Roger takes us on a universal search for the meaning of life. Then he shows us that it may have been right in front of us all along."

—Justin Harding, professional fly-fishing
guide, Utah Pro Fly Fishing

"*My Best Friend's Funeral* will take you on a journey through the universal struggle of youth, first love, addiction, loss, marriage, the highs and lows of adult life, fatherhood, finding God, and the untimely death of a best friend. Roger's openness will leave you stretched and challenged to live a life of sincerity and honest humility. In these pages is a beautiful roadmap of how to do friendship well. This story will move your heart in a very deep way, and leave you with much to consider."

—Charlotte Crotty, long-time friend

"My friend Roger writes a captivating, raw, touching memoir. It will make you laugh and cry, and cause you to regard your friendships as the greater gifts they are."

—BRITT MERRICK, FOUNDING PASTOR OF REALITY
CHURCH AND AUTHOR OF *Big God* AND *Godspeed*

"Enter this book. Please. Take yourself and enter. For from within it you will know what the Celts knew, how to be *Anam Cara*. *Anam* is the Gaelic word for soul; *cara* is the word for friend, together they equal soul friend. Lost are the days of 'soul friends' in our contemporary life, lost are those friendships that cut across all convention and category, friendships that convey deep recognition and belonging, friendships that see each other as whole people and help each other become whole and better versions of themselves. This book, these lives, they teach us, challenge us, carry us, and renew us once again toward the soulfulness of friendship. I know this to be true, for I was taught personally, and so can you. Read."

—GREG RUSSINGER, FRIEND OF TIM AND ROGER, AND
FOUNDING PASTOR OF THE BRIDGE COMMUNITY WHERE TIM
SERVED, LOVED, AND TAUGHT US TO BE SOUL FRIENDS

"A beautiful and brave tribute; casting light onto what it means to grieve and process the monumental loss of a parent and a best friend. I was engrossed by Roger's forthright writing; he lays himself bare about the things that we grapple with the most. What happens when we lose people we care about? What do we do next? Affirming, spiritual without being preachy, and above all, honest. Kudos."

—MARIO CALIRE, MULTI GRAMMY-WINNING
DRUMMER (WALLFLOWERS, OZOMATLI)

"Taut with the suspense of life itself, hung precariously between dark winter and brimming springtide. Like the Psalms, it shimmers with both sorrow and hope. The journey is lyrical, haunting, deeply personal yet rich in treasures for all. Amidst it all, Roger Thompson reminds us that the place of our greatest ache can be also the source of the greatest gift God gives others through us."

—JEDD MEDEFIND, PRESIDENT OF THE CHRISTIAN ALLIANCE
FOR ORPHANS AND AUTHOR OF *Becoming Home*

"I could not put this book down! A refreshingly raw, honest, insightful behind the scenes look into a friendship that God worked through to impact this entire generation! Each of our lives are difficult at times but reading this book reminded me of how God uses our pain and suffering to draw us closer to Him and to refine us so we can shine brighter."

—BRYAN JENNINGS, FOUNDER OF WALKING ON WATER

"This is a beautiful book about friendship, failure, and fighting with God and others over life's mysteries. Roger provides the reader a poetic, playful, and generous place to marinate in the experiences that flavor our lives. His stories moved me deeply, not only because of his engaging and humorous wit, but because I had the incredible privilege of sharing some of these memories with Roger and Tim. You will be encouraged by Roger's vulnerability and authenticity, and invited to open up your heart a little more to love and be loved."

—SCOTT GRABENDIKE, SENIOR PASTOR OF WESTBROOK CHURCH

my best friend's funeral

my best friend's funeral

a memoir

ROGER W. THOMPSON

NELSON
BOOKS

An Imprint of Thomas Nelson

© 2014 by Roger W. Thompson

All rights reserved. No portion of this book may be reproduced, stored in a retrieval system, or transmitted in any form or by any means—electronic, mechanical, photocopy, recording, scanning, or other—except for brief quotations in critical reviews or articles, without the prior written permission of the publisher.

Published in Nashville, Tennessee, by Nelson Books, an imprint of Thomas Nelson. Nelson Books and Thomas Nelson are registered trademarks of HarperCollins Christian Publishing, Inc.

The back cover photo was taken by Jesse Giglio. Interior photos came from the author's memory box. All interior artwork, sketches, and diagrams were provided by the author's mother.

Thomas Nelson titles may be purchased in bulk for educational, business, fundraising, or sales promotional use. For information, please e-mail SpecialMarkets@ ThomasNelson.com.

**Library of Congress Cataloging-in-Publication Data
is on file with the Library of Congress**

ISBN 9781400206131

Printed in the United States of America

14 15 16 17 18 RRD 6 5 4 3 2 1

*In memory of Paul Thompson
and Tim Garrety*

Contents

CONTENTS

Note from the Author

I HAVE AN ONGOING FEAR OF HAVING MY TIRES SLASHED. It's happened before. There was a girl I had a crush on in college who was also liked by a competitive list of others, many of whom were athletic stars on a variety of sports teams. I was not. So I played a different angle. As I made my pitch to her, I found myself editing my life through a set of filters I thought would increase my odds. I was in a band. I rode a motorcycle. I had awesome hair. It was all true.

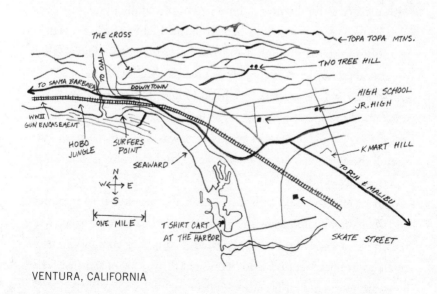

VENTURA, CALIFORNIA

There was a longer list of less cool things about me, however, all equally true, that didn't make the presentation. What I remember most about our first date was the next morning seeing a half-inch slash in the back tire of my motorcycle. I would like to think it was because I made some soccer player jealous. But it could have been because she found out I wasn't the lead singer.

Writing a book like this has similar risks. Our memories are imperfect, recalled through a process similar to making a cup of coffee. Bitter and undrinkable at first, as the beans are ground down, boiled over, and run through a set of filters, they become drinkable. And shareable. I wrote these stories because I missed my friend and through the writing he was back for a while. He was recalled through filters of a flawed memory, refined through furnaces of grief, and for a moment we were once again laughing and playing music and paddling our surfboards into the sunset. Now those stories are about to be shared.

Sharing stories requires an act of trust. You trust me to be truthful with the stories I tell (and not bore you unmercifully in the process). And I trust you to give me the benefit of the doubt as I piece together memories scattered through decades-old corners of my mind. I tried to write these stories as accurately as possible, but by nature of storytelling there will be some license I had to take. For example, early on it occurred to me as I wrote dialogue between Tim and me that there was no way I could remember exactly what was said so many years ago. I recall the emotions, the times and places, and the conversations, but not the exact words.

In an effort to deal with this, I created a panel of friends, along with Tim's family, to review these stories and make sure his voice was remembered correctly. I've also created a couple of composite characters to protect identities and because at forty years old, it just feels awkward to call old girlfriends.

But the events are true. As are the feelings they inspired. At times they may be more of an Instagram treatment than an exact photo. I've tried to write things as I remembered, or more honestly, as I felt them. For though we can't always recall the exact words that shaped who we are, we can recall the feeling of being shaped. That is what I've tried to do here.

I live in the town where most of these stories take place. I grew up with Tim here. I married here. I'm raising my sons here. I anticipate running into people at the store or at the beach who will inevitably correct me on some facts in this book, or accuse me of filtering the scenes. When they do, I will apologize and assure them that any omission or changing of a fact was due to limitations of memory and efforts to protect the privacy of those who did not choose to be a part of this book. Or to protect me from having my tires slashed.

ONE

In Search of a Father

"Why do men like me want sons?" he wondered. "It must be because they hope in their poor beaten souls that these new men, who are their blood, will do the thing they were not strong enough nor wise enough nor brave enough to do. It is rather like another chance at life; like a new bag of coins at a table of luck after your fortune is gone."

—JOHN STEINBECK, FROM *Cup of Gold*

CHAPTER 1

sold out

I FELL IN LOVE WITH MUSIC WHILE RIDING SHOTGUN DOWN an empty Western highway. It was in a faded blue '57 Chevy Apache pickup truck, presumably named after the Indians who wandered these roads before they were roads. From the running board, I used to climb into the wood-lined bed to watch dirt-track races on the long summer evenings of my youth.

Dad was driving, and sitting next to him on those desolate roads I always thought he seemed at his best. Windows down, he drove with one elbow resting on the windowsill, hand holding a cigarette. His other hand alternated between the wheel and the radio, tuning in highway poetry. My hand stretched out the passenger window, surfing the rise and fall of the Western wind as it flowed over the curve of the hood, along the fenders and through my fingers on its way to eternity. On the curl of the wind rode the scents of licorice weed and Marlboro Reds. We had found a back road to heaven, and with the full glory of Southern rock, we drove to the rhythm of the road.

Dad loved to sing when he drove. He would sing so loud I began to only recognize the songs through his voice. The soundtrack to his life fit the roads he traveled. The Allman Brothers, the Eagles, Bob Dylan, Jim Croce, the Band. His favorite songs seemed to be about going somewhere, about a journey. They were a roadmap to a place in his soul that could only be found through the music. At a time when nothing made sense in his world, this music was a compass and a salve for wounds inflicted by the troubles of his generation.

In addition to memorizing times tables and state capitals, I memorized the words to "Hotel California" so I could sing along as we drove. The opening lines sang like a promise of what was to come. "On a dark desert highway, cool wind in my hair."

Along the twists and turns of the Sierra Nevada foothills we'd sing harmony with Don Henley. As we sang, Dad was happy, and I was happy. The sound of my little voice inside his made me feel safe.

By grade school these harmonies had disappeared, and sadness made itself at home in my heart. Dad and I didn't sing together anymore. It was during this time I got my first guitar. From the moment I held it, I imagined myself in a band writing songs that could make it all better. We moved a lot in those years, and though I don't remember what happened to the guitar, the songs kept writing themselves into my soul. By the time we moved back to the beach town I was born in, the songs were ready to come out. I just needed someone to help me find a rhythm. It would be a lifelong friendship with Tim Garrety that would help me discover it.

Music has etched memories in my mind, like grooves of a record. I can't remember the name of the girl I first danced with in the sixth grade, but I remember the song was "Time After Time." I'll also never forget the beach where I was hanging out when I heard my first Violent Femmes song. It was the day I got into my first fistfight. By then Tim and I were good friends and spending another summer day together at the beach.

We were sitting on the short brick wall between the sand and the street, awaiting a ride from my grandma, when a tanned, scrawny kid approached us. He was smaller than us but had several friends with him.

Still, their collective weight looked to be only 150 pounds. He stood as close as he could and with as much anger as an upper-middle-class white kid from the beach could summon, gestured with his fists to my face.

"What are you doing here? This is *our* beach."

Tim stepped in front of me and threw him over the wall. He wasn't a very good negotiator. All of a sudden more kids surrounded us and we all started punching and kicking and cussing. We created a sandstorm and through the billowing clouds of dust, arms and legs flailed wildly in the air while "Add It Up" from Violent Femmes blasted in the background. I imagine it's what a fight between Snoopy and Pig-Pen would have looked like on a Charlie Brown TV special.

Just when it looked like we might be overrun by this pack of wild beach Orcs, my five-foot grandma pulled up in the getaway Town Car. With our boogie boards in the trunk and us in the backseat, we sped off down the street with Tim's middle finger out the window getting the last word.

This and most other memories of my youth are played out over a background of music. I can still sing along with every word of "Hotel California" and if I'm alone on the road, arm surfing out the window, I can still hear my father's voice in the harmony.

Generations are defined by music, further subdivided by genres and styles. The kids in our high school quad were organized like sections of a record shop. Pop, punk, alternative, show tunes, and so forth. By high school Tim and I had been best friends for years and during our freshman year, my childhood dream was realized when we started our first band.

It was a punk band we named Common Indecency, and our music lived up to the name. He played drums and I played bass. Early on I learned to lock into his beat and bounce a riff against his kick drum. We developed a timing and style that would go far beyond the music. Eventually outgrowing the garage, we converted his parents' tool shed into a music room, complete with egg-crate walls and neon beer signs, and in that holy space wrote the soundtrack of our lives.

Soon we were legitimately playing venues that previously we had to sneak into. After gigs we would hang out in all-night diners with our tight group of friends, discussing music, life, and lesser things. When we were not playing, we were going to as many shows as possible. There were lots of local venues where we could hear music, but when it was Social Distortion or Pearl Jam, we went to the Ventura Theater. For the high school music connoisseur, the place was a temple and we would sit at the altar of our music gods memorizing every beat or riff that came from the stage.

The marquee read like Greek mythology, and we imagined our name suspended in that immortal space above the street. That became our dream. Rolling up to the Ventura Theater, name on the marquee, looking out the tinted windows of our tour bus at the line of people waiting to watch us play on that stage.

A short lifetime later, I rounded the corner from Main Street on my way to the theater with these thoughts running through my head. Tim and I had been best friends since childhood, and now I was staring at his name in that magical space. No local opening bands. Nothing about what shows were coming up next week. Just simple black letters against a white, backlit marquee.

TIM

Below it, a line formed, running past the row of Harleys in front and then wrapping around the block. I watched through dark-tinted glass the people in line, staring back at us. But instead of the dream tour bus scenario I had always imagined, I was looking through some beat-up Ray-Bans, delivering my best friend's wife to his funeral.

She looked strong and beautiful and pale, and I couldn't look her in the eyes. So as we parked I distracted myself by looking at the line that continued to grow longer than lines of any shows in my memories.

It was strange to me how few of the people I recognized. Up until a few days before, Tim and I had spent more than two decades together, and I assumed I would know most of the people he knew. Or at least recognize them. I couldn't help but wonder who would be in line if it were my name on the marquee. What kind of a life makes enough difference for this many people that they would wait for hours to have one last chance to be near a person?

This question sank in deep, and I didn't realize how much it would haunt my life, until it eventually transformed it. Just the thought of this question made me feel like I was falling short on a test I knew I could have passed if I'd only gone to the library instead of the beach. Only this test was life. In the back alley of the theater, next to the trash can that smelled like urine and stale beer, with a line of strangers staring at the concrete, I felt a distantly familiar stir in my soul. Then a question whispered like thunder.

Are you living a life that matters?

Closing my eyes to fight back the fear of what was next, I heard the question again. Only this time it sounded more like the voice of my best friend.

———————

Best friends are like mirrors, helping us see around the blind spots of our lives. Sometimes they are those annoying dressing-room mirrors that let you see how the pants look from behind—but you never really see how the pants fit because all you can look at is that bald spot on the top of your head; you just stand there wondering how it got there and why it's the second-fastest-growing area of your body. But if your best friend is seeing the worst angle of you and is still a great friend, there is hope. Because at least one person on earth who doesn't have to care for you, does.

That person can gently (or directly) point out those most important areas of your character that could and should be better. Then, best friends become backstage mirrors surrounded by lights, illuminating the possibilities of a better self. So maybe I shouldn't have been surprised that at the earthly end of my friendship with Tim, I was still seeing myself reflected in him. Or that he was revealing the gap between who I was and who I could be.

Either way, it made me angry.

Here I was getting ready to deliver a eulogy for someone I'd spent most of my life with, and I was being reminded, minutes before, how inadequate I was to deliver it. Not just because every time I had to say something in front of a crowd it made me panic uncontrollably, but because each line I was about to say was a checklist of my own deficiencies. That line about loving . . . I need to love better. About serving others . . . I mostly avoid them. About being a good friend . . . here I was at his funeral mostly thinking of myself and how the people in the balcony were going to get a great view of my bald spot as I spoke. The same one he never mentioned.

Perhaps that's the point. That those great lives lived among us are mirrors reflecting light into our darkness. And the more briefly they shine, the more urgently they get our attention. They remind us that every moment is both a gift and a call to action. That in any moment, I could begin to rewrite my life for the eulogy that will someday be given for me. Backstage that night, it occurred to me for the first time that I was also about to hold up a mirror to all those standing in line. I was about to reveal to them, through a life that had ended, through a vulnerable and broken messenger, that all of us together have just this one chance to become what we were born to be.

Backstage, the greenroom wasn't as cool as I'd imagined. I had images in my mind, all in black and white, of our band sitting around the greenroom, talking about the tour with other bands and about how the sound guy in Spokane was tone deaf and the salsa in Madison was just some ketchup mixed with mayonnaise. We would be smoking too. I had smoked a couple of times as a teenager and looked like a penguin in a knife fight. I couldn't figure out which hand should hold the cigarette, and I was always nervous that I was about to set myself on fire. But in black and white, we'd look cool and I'd be asking Flea from the Red Hot Chili Peppers for a light. As he was handing it to me, he would be saying how much he liked the bass riff on that song I wrote about the girl I never asked out in college.

From the greenroom I could watch as people poured in. Family in front. Balcony jammed with the underage crowd. High school friends disappointedly gathered around a dry bar, looking like they needed a drink. It felt more reunion tour than funeral. I imagined all the black shirts as concert tees with a list of things on the back like, "He helped me fix my faucet" and "He drove me to the airport" and "He talked me down from the ledge." For a moment, life pushed back death. Friends were being reunited. There were conversations about old times. Even laughter. They kept pouring in.

I was on after the worship band, after our mentor, and before the video with the Green Day song, "Time of Your Life." There's a cadence coded into grief that takes over when our hearts fail. In times like this, we march instinctively to its beat. Over the last several days, it had become a comfort of sorts; and now, while I was sitting between a pile of cables and a piano on the hardwood stage, it provided a moment of quiet.

Then it got loud. The band was onstage. The audience began to move and the theater sprang to life. But instead of lighters waving, there were hands. Grasping and groping. Pleading for something or someone to come into the theater and make sense of it all. To turn back time.

This wasn't how it was supposed to happen. This was supposed to be our opening band onstage. We were supposed to be in the greenroom laughing and flicking ashes into ashtrays. We should have been quoting Nietzsche and Nirvana and debating the virtues of three-quarter timing. There should have been laughing and singing in the triumphant splendor of our youth. But life is sometimes a ten-thousand-piece puzzle of the sky with no edge pieces. In a few moments, I would need to put it together for that theater full of people.

The worship band led in, and the crowd responded with raised hands and closed eyes. I never shut my eyes when I sing. Someone once told me the reason you shut your eyes while singing is to block out all distractions and be totally abandoned to the moment. Only then can God have complete access to your heart. I tried it once, but I kept thinking someone was going to sneak up from behind. So I stopped. Now God has to find other ways into my heart, and since I always have my eyes open, that has been difficult to do. Even for God.

But this time, by the third song, I realized my eyes were shut. I was totally abandoned. Then as my hands lifted, new access was given to my heart and God moved in to expand it like a water balloon, until I was sure it would pop and anybody around would be drenched with its contents. But instead of filling with peace, it was filling with pain, which flooded in until there was no room for anything else. It pushed out all remaining hope or courage or air, and I began to drown. The only hope of breathing would be to let it pop. My vulnerability has purposely been limited to small groups in quiet places, but here I was onstage, in front of a crowd that, with the exception of only a few, would never have known I had any emotions at all.

Death creates an unexpected capacity of feeling, and I was able to feel every word our mentor Jeff was now onstage saying. He talked of the sounds of Skate Street, the skate park he, Tim, and I had created after an idea at a backyard barbecue. They were sounds of a vision we erected from piles of plywood and two-by-fours. A day earlier, Jeff and I walked through the skate park trying to decide what was next. Where there were usually sounds of wheels on ramps—grinding, sliding, and rolling—there was silence. Behind the silence there was emptiness. Behind the emptiness there was pain. The same pain I felt now as he spoke of what once was, and what would never be.

As he finished onstage, time slowed and then stood still. It was my turn. A bunch of still-frame images flashed through my mind. Our picture before the seventh-grade dance. At the beach. In the back of Spanish class. High school graduation. College graduation. The band. The skate park. Weddings. Kids. Lifeless in a casket. My heart continued to expand out of my chest until it finally popped. There I stood, alone onstage, exposed, in a puddle of hopelessness and fear.

Not long before he died, Tim visited me in Nashville to see Rocketown, an entertainment venue I helped design and was then running. It was a 2.0 version of what we had built back home. In addition to a skate park—and the coffee shop conveniently located outside my office—it included a live music venue. Though it was arguably the best venue in town, we floundered after opening, struggling to get anybody to come to shows.

We did great promotions, experimented with different prices, and did everything the experts suggested. We even prayed. But nothing would fill the venue until we discovered a simple and obvious key to filling it every time. In order for anybody to show up, they had to love the band. If the band didn't have fans, there was nothing you could do to get people to hear them play. If they did, you couldn't beat them away. They came because there was something about the music that connected on such a visceral level that not being there would be like not breathing.

I came to realize, no matter the style of music, that people love different bands for the same reasons. The music is inspiring or it helps during difficult times or it speaks truth when nobody else will—in a way that makes sense. This is the music that matters. When this music was offered on our stage, the venue would fill with people who wanted it. Or needed it. When word got out that we had music people wanted, our venue went from regularly empty to regularly sold-out. In Nashville there were lots of shows, but the ones that mattered, the ones that were talked about on Monday, were played to sold-out crowds.

Looking over the audience, I couldn't help but wonder what kind of life you have to live to sell out the Ventura Theater. To sell it out in only five days, with nothing more than word-of-mouth promotion. No radio. No flyers stapled to telephone poles. No advertisements in the free newspapers at coffee shops on the pages next to the editorials about how legalizing marijuana would be good for the economy.

That stage represented a promise of everything that could have been. To our young selves, being elevated there for a single ephemeral moment would have meant we had made it in life. That the music we made, made a difference. That we would not be soon forgotten.

I had been trying to write a eulogy that got to the secret of what really matters in the end. Of what could possibly make sense of this senselessness called life. It turns out the answer is a path we all know but have allowed the dandelions and weeds to hide from us. In the end, it's not really a secret at all. It just takes a life well lived to clear the way.

The lights dimmed as I approached the microphone, and for a moment I was eighteen again, thinking about my opening riff and waiting for a stick count to launch into everything that was supposed to be. Empty Western highways. Backyards and baseball. White picket fences. Anniversaries. Bicycles left in the driveway. Gray beards. Friends to share the music with, even if the music had grown too loud.

It had been more than ten years since our band last played. Until the last few days before the funeral, that music had been long forgotten. Practicality had displaced the dreams. Of all the things there were to remember about our friendship in the end, I wondered why it would be the music.

Then it came to me.

On this day of my greatest brokenness, standing in front of a sold-out theater at my best friend's funeral, our dream was fulfilled because Tim was a musician in a life filled with noise. He didn't just pump out a radio single; he gave us a short lifetime of albums recorded on vinyl, richly textured, adding to the canon of timeless music that forever enriches our lives. The crowd was here to listen to one last song. They were here because they were fans, and to not be here would be like not breathing. They were here because they loved the music. This was his encore.

Then somehow, at the hands of a master musician, the moment became like a song you still find yourself singing when the music has stopped.

Standing in silence, I pulled out paper covered with words I'd written to sum up the life of one I loved. For the past five days, those words had been full of anguish and anger. They now read like a song list. They revealed how to sell out the Ventura Theater. And how to live a life that matters. In his leaving, my best friend gave a parting gift: a few words to help guide us toward our better selves. To become who we were meant to be.

The lights came on. Stepping up to the mic, I heard a four-count rhythm in my soul, then began.

"Thank you for letting me say a few words about our beloved friend."

CHAPTER 2

the road home

IT WAS LATE, SO I WAS STARTLED WHEN THE PHONE RANG.

"Hello?"

"Hey, Rog, it's Tim. Are you around tomorrow? Let's grab some coffee at Simone's."

I had some news I couldn't wait to share with him, so I was excited that we were getting together. My wife and I recently moved back home with our one-and-a-half-year-old son after being in Nashville for a few years. Although Tim and I had already seen each other a number of times, we still hadn't had a chance to do the deep catching up we needed to. When we did see each other, there was an air of expectancy, like a forgotten word on the tip of a tongue, so I knew we were due.

As I walked into the coffee shop, he was tucked into the niche in back, deep in a cushioned chair, writing busily into a well-worn journal. As he noticed my arrival and stood up, I just jumped right in.

"It's a boy! Number two!"

He beamed that familiar smile, grabbed my shoulders, smiled even bigger, then pulled me in for the "this-is-the-best-news-ever" embrace. It was our second son, and by his reaction you would have thought it was his. As we settled into the chairs, we got through the routine of catching up pretty quickly. Being friends for as long as we had been, it was more like auto-syncing a computer and iPad.

The conversation we were moving into, though, was more about realigning our envisioned future. For most of our lives, we'd created the lifestyle we wanted out of the strength of collective vision. I'd only been home for three months, and much of that time was spent getting settled back into the house and into a new job. So I was living in an unusually present-centered state of mind and was ready to dream again. So was he.

We had just celebrated our birthdays. He was twenty-one days older than me, which, he liked to remind me, was why he was so much smarter. Not long before, we would celebrate our birthdays by ditching work to go snowboarding. But now with kids and responsibilities we were lucky to ditch bedtime stories for a beer. His son turned three just before we returned home to Ventura, and I couldn't believe he was that old. It was the first startling reminder of how quickly life passes. It seemed as though he had been born, I went away for a few days, and now he had a better vocabulary than I did. It was probably because his dad was twenty-one days older than me.

"I tore apart the skate park. It's time for 3.0."

This was exciting news. We opened the skate park around our twenty-fifth birthdays and during the last eight years had done two major redesigns of the ramps. Like anything else, styles and tastes of skateboarding change over time. In order to remain relevant you have to constantly be out in front. We revolutionized the skate park industry with the opening of Skate Street by bending the rules of plywood, and everything else with it. Our vision and imagination led us to possibilities previously never considered—and it was time to do that again. He was just waiting for me. Together we were unstoppable.

This next iteration would be the culmination of our collective experiences, of what he learned over the past three years and what I learned at Rocketown. But it would also be centered on the core of what we had started. Sort of a "third verse, same as the first." More important, it would be another chance for our friendship to reunite and build something significant. It was these projects that brought out our best and neither of us could wait to get started. In many ways, this conversation about the future made it feel like I had finally come home.

This was how we built our friendship. It was our way to engage with the world and to squeeze out all that was possible. We somehow came to believe that anything we could dream up was achievable, and since the seventh grade we'd dreamt up one possibility after the next. It wasn't blood brothers or pinky swears but something deeper. As if God revealed to us a future version of the world only made possible through the deep bonds of our friendship and the shared burden of seeing it come true.

At a chapel service my freshman year of college at Westmont, I first heard the story from the Bible about the guys who cut a hole in a roof to lower their friend down so Jesus could heal him. I wasn't that into chapel; during four years of college the only other one I remember is when my friend Alden lost a bet and had to go to chapel wearing his wetsuit. So it's surprising how well I remembered this particular story.

There were these four guys who had a paralyzed friend and wanted him to walk again. They heard talk of a man who could heal visiting a house nearby, so they threw their buddy on a mat and carried him there. But when they arrived, such a large crowd had gathered that there was no way to get to the front door. These four guys, who had been carrying their paralyzed friend for who knows how far, couldn't get in.

At the time of that chapel service, I was obsessed with snowboarding, so I tried to picture him paralyzed by a snowboarding accident. But then I thought there couldn't be any snow near the Dead Sea, or wherever it was that Jesus liked to hang out. Maybe it was donkey racing. Either way, it didn't really matter, because there was no way those guys were going to see Jesus that day. They got turned away, but one of the friends must have been determined to have his buddy healed.

Rather than heading home, someone came up with the bright idea of climbing onto the roof, getting their paralyzed friend up there, then busting a hole through the ceiling above Jesus' head. I imagine they all looked at one another and shrugged their shoulders and said, "Cool." So they got up there, cut out a hole, and lowered him down in front of the crowd. And he was healed. The Bible said it was because of the faith of his friends. I think it was also because of their *cojones*.

In the back of the bleachers of our school's gymnasium, I listened to the chaplain talk about the importance of true friendship and give a word picture of what this kind of friendship looked like. In our lifetime, he went on to say, these friendships would get us through the things we couldn't get through alone. The investments we made into friendships now would pay out over our lives.

As hard as it was to imagine the kind of difficulties that would come my way, I had already seen enough life to know the value of a friend. It wasn't lost on me that at the beginning of our college experience, rather than talking about the importance of studying or getting involved in the school, the chaplain was encouraging us to find the kind of friends who would carry the mat. Tim was that kind of friend. He would even be the one to climb the wall and bust through the roof.

Over coffee at Simone's we were catching up on life when the subject of work came up.

"So, how's your new job going?"

"Dude, I don't know what I'm doing."

"That's never stopped you before."

He was right. I've always succeeded most when I didn't know what couldn't be done. I learned that from him.

"I have to fly to Florida tomorrow. I have some meetings somewhere on the beach outside of Pensacola."

"Cool. Let's get started on 3.0 when you get back."

After the excitement of this conversation I really didn't want to leave, but the prospect of some downtime on the beach to do some dreaming about our future made it tolerable.

As observed through the front window of a rental car, the coastline of the Florida panhandle is an endless miniature golf course weaving through waterslides and tacky high-rise hotels. Occasionally, through a clearing, you can glimpse the white sands and crystal-clear water that everybody comes to that area to see. My new job was with a book publisher, and I was on this trip pursuing a potential author lead. Only I was as confused about my new job (and life in general) as some of these land developers were about how to recreate the hillside villas of Italy on the Florida Gulf.

I had time to kill before my dinner meeting, so I thought I'd go for a walk along the beach and jump in the water. I have traveled the world over, but I have never experienced sand so pure or soft underfoot. The purity gave my feet something to grasp; each step was reluctant to let go of the ground, creating small *swoosh* sounds as the arches of my feet flexed their way to the water's edge. The snow-white sand sparkling around my toes originated from mountain peaks of an earlier period. Through time and struggle, water wore down the Appalachian mountains and carried with it rich deposits of minerals to the panhandle coast. Then, over time, the ocean continued the process until it produced the perfection it desired: pure, crystal quartz—the most beautiful sand in the world. It's the constant grinding that creates purity.

As I swam out, the sun reflected through the water and off the ocean floor, magnifying everything in sight below the surface. The colors of the fish. The details of the sand. The confusion in my life. Was I really back home to do something new with Tim? Was it time for us to take our dreams to the next level? Or was I supposed to be in this new job and support him from a distance?

Floating in clear waters of the Florida Gulf, I concluded that the purpose I was looking for would be revealed through our shared destiny. And I was comforted to know that Tim was there to help sort it out. I would start by calling him after my meeting to continue the conversation we began at the coffee shop. With clarity and excitement, I swam ashore, grabbed my towel, and headed to the hotel to get ready for my meeting.

The meeting was at a crab shack right on the beach. It was the kind of place where you would expect to find Jimmy Buffet drinking a domestic beer at a bar lit up with old-school Christmas lights and neon signs. I felt right at home.

The roots of this trip started to grow several months earlier back in Nashville when I was talking with my friend Jay. Jay has been one of those people in my life whom I seldom get to see, but he improves my life each time I do. He was an emerging church leader at the time, and as such was connected to others like him. Every year a group of them gathered privately on the Florida Gulf to discuss the future of the world and how the church might better prepare itself to meet it. One of the guys present happened to be someone my new company was interested in publishing, so Jay set up this introduction dinner.

As we got started, I was distracted by my last conversation with Tim and the clarity that emerged in the water. I was also distracted by my phone ringing nonstop. I tried to play it off like it was normal. That I was an important guy all sorts of people wanted to connect with. Just like this guy should. In reality it was Dan calling. Dan was a longtime friend of mine and Tim's. I assumed he probably just wanted to catch up, so I kept bouncing his calls and got my head back into the meeting.

In spite of these distractions—or maybe because of—the meeting went very well. To celebrate, I grabbed a beer from the neon-lit bar and headed to the beach to watch the sun set over the Gulf. Sunsets have always felt like a fireworks ending to a good day. As the fiery fingers of pink, orange, and red stretched across the sky, my soul celebrated a reawakening. Confusion had turned to clarity, and soon I'd be on the phone with my best friend confirming our shared vision and making plans to launch our new future.

A few hours later, as I pulled into the parking lot of the hotel, I finally picked up my buzzing phone. It was Dan again.

"Roger, you need to sit down."

There was a lone bench on the edge of the parking lot lit by the soft glow of a street lamp. Everything around it was dark. I sat down. He began to talk and I heard a crack in the universe. Then everything went blank.

I had forgotten why I had come here and what I was doing. Shortly after, I forgot where I was. Stumbling through the door of my hotel room reminded me that I was in Florida. On the beach in Florida. That would be enough for now. I knew I would need to get home in the next twenty-four hours, and at least knowing where I was would be a good starting point.

I suddenly felt sick and tried making it to the bathroom, but I fell before I got there. After another attempt I was back down, so I just stayed on the floor and shut my eyes, trying to get the room to stand still. Eventually I gathered enough strength to pull myself into a chair and bury my head in my hands, but I couldn't quite feel anything. My hands were as numb as my head. Though I could consciously force them to rub my eyes, it felt like there was a brick between them. So there I sat until the brick in my hands told my legs it was time to get up. When I finally reached the bathroom, I stuck my head in the sink. Then over the toilet. And back and forth until there was nothing left inside.

Things were beginning to come to me now. I was here to put a deal together. I swam in the Gulf. I ate crab at a shack on the beach. I had a beer as the sun went down. It was a beautiful sunset. I had just parked the car at the hotel. Dan kept calling. He called again. I answered. He told me to sit down. I found a bench at a dark edge of the parking lot. I sat. There was silence. He said Tim was dead.

The room began spinning again until there was no way to control it. Then something deep inside started to make its way out. It was fear's defeat over faith, taking control of my body, causing convulsions that resembled a hangover from a long night of drinking away the world. The convulsions knocked me to my hands and knees. When I tried to crawl to safety, a second attack knocked me to the floor. Semi-conscious, I lay with half my body in the bathroom with fingers clawing at the carpet outside of it, trying to pull myself out of the foxhole before the grenade finished me off.

Eventually I was able to push off the floor, crawl to the door of the hotel room, and use the doorknob to pull myself to my feet. With the room still spinning, I slowly opened the door and stumbled into the night. The sound of waves was soothingly familiar, so I followed that sound until I reached a stretch of sand reflecting the silver light of the moon. Somewhat revived by the salty air, I was able to think a little.

I needed to get home. Beyond that, things were blurry, but at least I knew what I needed to do next. Then I sat. And I cried. I cried alone through the night. Alone through the darkness. I cried until the moon disappeared beyond the horizon and the whole world faded to black.

"I need to catch the next plane out."

My head knew what to do but my quivering voice could barely get the words over the phone.

"Sir, are you okay?"

"Yes . . . no."

A preprogrammed set of controls took over my body, and somehow I went through the motions of getting back to the airport and onto a plane. There was a transfer in Houston where I tried to order some coffee, but I couldn't remember my drink. Ten years earlier Tim and I got hooked on coffee while building the skate park. We could work all night and, instead of sleeping, pound a coffee drink and keep on working. I'd been drinking the same thing every morning since. More than thirty-six hundred coffee orders later, standing at the Starbucks in the Houston Hobby airport, I couldn't remember what my drink was. Somehow I ended up with a soy latte. Which wasn't very helpful at all.

The drive between the Los Angeles airport and home in Ventura winds north along the coast of Malibu, alongside some of my favorite beaches. For me it's the road home. After high school, Tim and I worked at some of these beaches as members of the beach patrol. The universe somehow deemed a handful of us worthy enough to have the best job on earth. We were hired by the owners of multimillion-dollar beach homes to sit in front of their houses, mostly vacation homes, just to make sure nobody climbed onto their properties to find a bathroom.

And since the private beaches of northern Malibu were so fraught with danger, we had to work in pairs. So Tim and I took turns surfing. When there weren't any waves, we resorted to just playing Frisbee on the beach. When duty called, we would kick the unsuspecting public off the private property above the official land marker of median-high tide. I bought a lot of guitar amps with the money earned on those beaches.

As I was driving along this familiar stretch of coastline, Dan called again, so I pulled into the parking lot at Matador Beach—the one where Tim and I spent most our time. He gave me more details about what had happened. Tim had been on his Harley only a couple of miles from home, riding with the sun at his back. The car never saw him. Details came in like a list of facts. There would be a gathering tomorrow. A viewing was in the works. The memorial would be at the Ventura Theater. A date was set. The moon is 238,855 miles from earth. As I got off the phone the reality hit me, and I had to get out to walk around. A little while later, Dan called back to ask if I knew what I would be saying at the memorial.

Sometime on the beach the night before it had crossed my mind, but I hadn't thought about what I would say. I hadn't even gotten home yet. In less than twenty-four hours I had to make the switch of thinking about the future we were still creating to thinking about the life we had. I had to switch to past tense. Tim was on the road home. Maybe we all are.

I found a picnic bench on the bluff above the beach and sat to watch the sun lower itself over the Pacific. There is nothing in this life that prepares you to write a memorial speech for your best friend. I had no idea where to start. So I started at the beginning.

"Thank you for letting me say a few words about our beloved friend. I had the privilege of being Tim's closest friend for over twenty years. I got to know him the same way a lot of you did. I was new in town and had a bit of a troubled past . . ."

CHAPTER 3

secret fishing
hole, part one

SOME OF THE BEST DAYS OF MY LIFE HAVE BEEN SPENT FISHING
and not catching any fish. I learned to fish at our family's cabin, which
is snuggled in hundred-year-old pine trees on the western slope of
the Sierra Nevada mountains. Visible from old wicker chairs on the
covered porch were endless mountains and ridgelines, all reflected in
the lake below.

My family has been coming to this lake for generations, and much
of my memory is recorded along its shore. Each rock and stump and
dock presents in my mind a faded photo of my sister and me jumping in the lake, learning to build a snowman, or proudly posing with
a fish almost as big as our smiles. The infiniteness of the mountains
shaped adventures of imagination while the quietness of the lake gently nursed the scrapes and bruises of my heart.

In the cabin next to us lived an old man named Barney. He
looked exactly as you would expect. He was as old as the dirt he kept
his worms in, and he wore flannels over timeworn blue jeans that
sagged from behind, like Levi's did a design collaboration with gravity.
Though I'm sure he had several colors of flannel, in my memory they

are all checkered in red and black. He was a bit of a legend in these parts and knew everything about the fish in the lake as well as in the streams surrounding it. I was led to believe he knew each fish by name.

I would stare out the window until I could see Barney puttering around his garage, which I took as an invitation to come over and ask him everything he knew about fishing. And since he knew everything about fishing, I assumed he knew everything about life. If I was mad about school, or nervous that my dad wouldn't make it to the cabin this time, I would order all my questions just right in my head on the way to Barney's garage. But the only questions that ever came out were about how to catch a fish. He would look at me and pause and then draw a map in the dirt and give me some worms. Then he'd send me on my search.

Through woods and weeds I'd explore until I came to the place he intended, then carefully bait my hook and cast a line. And I wouldn't catch a thing. But as I'd reel in the line and wonder if I needed a new worm or should just cast to a different spot, my thoughts would focus more on the problem of how to catch fish and less on whatever I was bothered with before. Soon the world would drift away. Looking back, I'm pretty sure Barney knew the real questions I was asking.

I grew a little older, and I learned that the fish would rise for their evening meal in late summer evenings, when the shadows of the pines reached across the water to dance along the edges of the lake. From the water's edge, mountains stretched in every direction as far as I could see. At the end of each day the boats headed to their docks, the winds returned to their mountain passes, and in the stillness of the silence I would wonder about the world. *How far are those mountains? Can they be reached from here?*

Somehow I knew fishing would be better in the high country beyond. The mountains silhouetted in the sunset, the last light bending like arms giving the lake one last embrace before saying goodnight.

Then, in the eternal briefness of the twilight, I looked up and understood for the first time that I was a small child in the vastness of this wilderness. I would fish alone into the dark and then under a starlit sky, watching for shooting stars and wishing I was fishing with my dad.

Deep in the mountains, a river flows with the hopes of every boy who has longed for his dad to take him there. It's a secret fishing hole reached only on paths marked by a father's memory of traveling it before. As a boy stares in doubt, the father will step confidently on the path that leads to the right location. As they travel along, he explains that the path to the right leads to a section of water too close to the falls and the one to the left leads to a section of intoxicating beauty but has no fish. Together they walk under a canopy of aspens or willows or pines and talk about how to catch fish, how to avoid poison oak, and how to handle the constant tattling of Samantha who sits in the front of class. As they talk, the earth receives each new step softly underfoot.

The secret fishing hole is an oracle where fathers pass along the ancient wisdom needed to survive in this life. They scout the banks and teach their sons how to read the water. They point to the eddy behind the rock holding a large brown trout and to the seams in the current where food passes by. Fathers explain the importance of hitting a mark. That if you drift a fly on one side of the seam, the trout will rise, but if you are even slightly off target, it will be gone for good. If you hook into what you're hoping for, fathers teach how to use the current to reel it in. And they'll teach how to avoid the snags and the stumps you don't yet see.

My dad first told me about the secret fishing hole when I was six years old. He had just returned from the high country, and heavy in his hands was a white Styrofoam cooler he heaved like a treasure chest onto the paisley tablecloth on our tiny apartment kitchen table. He lifted the top, and my heart raced as he revealed more and bigger trout than I had ever seen.

They reminded me of fish I saw packed on ice in the discount grocery store, near where my mom picked up the ground beef. I used to stare into the fish case imagining those trout alive in the stream fighting against the end of my line. I would be fishing with my dad, and he would be sober, and I would be safe, and we would be stealing back the time stolen from us. Now, with a cooler of trout in our kitchen, my imagination ran wild with hope.

"Where did you catch these?"

"I found a secret fishing hole."

Dad seemed bigger as he spoke of what he found. He described the endless beauty of the high country and the discoveries made beyond the fear of the familiar. Through a meadow wound an unnamed river. It teemed with life so abundant; sections crossable from a standing leap held sixteen-inch trout below. Along these banks he had found a part of himself that had long been lost. A hero returning victorious from a long battle against his darkness, he was ready to lead his family toward a better future. Describing the scene, his heart wandered back, taking mine with it.

"Daddy?"

"Yes, son?"

"Can I go there?"

"When you're ready, we'll fish there together."

And for a while, everything was better.

CHAPTER 4

angel falls

IN THOSE YEARS WE WERE LIVING IN THE SOUTHERN SAN Joaquin Valley of California in a little town called Oildale, just north of Bakersfield. Dad found work in the oil patch surrounding the area, and we moved into a house on the edge of what was known as the Kern River oil field. During the time we lived there, it was the fifth-largest oil field in the country. It started just down the street and extended to the lower foothills of the Sierra Nevada mountains, where Dad liked to escape the heat to go fishing.

I have a portrait that my mom painted of him working in those fields. It was a hot day in late spring, and he was working in his undershirt, muscles exposed to challenge the elements. His hair was long, his face was chiseled, and he had a workingman's beard. Behind him was a patch of wildflowers. He possessed a great strength full of gentleness. I hung this painting in my college dorm room where others would say he looked like Jesus. To me, he felt like God.

On summer evenings we would often drive through the foothills just to put some distance on the day. Sometimes we would end up at the local speedway to watch dirt track races. We couldn't afford tickets, but there was a hill across from the track with a rutted dirt road to the top. Dad would stomp on the gas pedal and kick up a cloud of dust, trying to get enough momentum to make it up the hill before his cherished old engine would give out. We'd sit in the back of his beat-up Chevy pickup with blankets and whatever tools were left from working in these same foothills earlier in the day. It felt like we were above it all.

The announcer's voice would crackle distantly through the loud-speakers, and Dad would explain the rules of racing. The demolition races were my favorite. There was always one guy we would root for as he tried to make it through the obstacles with other cars trying to bash him and keep him from finishing the race. In some ways I could relate. And just hoped he made it out alive.

The first *Star Wars* had just come out in theaters, and the view over the foothills resembled a planet from the movie. It was completely barren. In place of anything natural were half-rusted oil rigs, drilling pads, and large industrial machines used to extract the remains of an ancient age. At the top of each hill were large metal tanks and steel towers. Below, pipes came out of the ground, crossed stretches of dirt, and returned beneath the surface. Scattered throughout was a lifeless forest of tar-covered poles connected with wires that also seemed to start and end below the dirt. Everything had some relationship to the dirt, or something below it.

It was a cityscape made of dirt and smoke and steel. Nothing could grow there. And nothing would live long if it did.

———————

At the end of our neighborhood's cul-de-sac was a high school, and beyond that an area known as the Sumps. A relic of the oil industry, it was once a place to trap oil being sucked out of the surrounding ground. From the sky it must have looked like a bunch of big dough-nuts made of dirt. A rusted chain-link fence surrounded the whole area, and it seemed to have no end.

I had stood at the border to look but was afraid to enter. Stories made their way through the neighborhood that the place was full of tar traps. It was like quicksand but scarier. If you got caught in one, you would slowly sink into a bottomless black abyss and suffocate with the dead dinosaurs. Walking alone along the edge of the Sumps, I saw some kids sneaking their bikes back out through a hole in the fence.

"What's in there?"

Their faces were red with adrenaline and they looked a little relieved that they made it out.

"It's so cool in there!"

"Yeah, and there are lots of jumps and snakes!"

"And huge hills to ride down!"

They didn't say anything about tar traps, but they probably didn't go that far back. I needed to get in there.

I needed a bike.

My first problem was that the bike I wanted was beyond our means. It was a JMC Black Shadow, chromed out, light and fast. The second problem was that once I decided I wanted something, there could be no substitute. Dad suggested I find a job. Luckily one of the afternoon papers needed a delivery boy in my neighborhood. It was a small enough paper that I could stuff a hundred of them into the double-sided cloth bags they gave me and still carry it over my shoulders. Though not old enough to work, my sister, Rachel, was willing to help me with anything and would often roll papers with me. At an early age we had already figured out how to bear the world together. Upon completion, the tightly rolled and rubber-banded papers were the perfect size for chucking.

I got so good I could nail any porch from only halfway up the driveway. I would sometimes wind up like Fernando Valenzuela, with a quick look to the sky to make sure God was watching, just for emphasis. This allowed me to deliver to a lot of houses quickly, which was important because I got paid in tips.

The people in my neighborhood didn't have much money, but everyone seemed to have a soft spot for a little paperboy trying to save up enough money to buy a bike. Except for Mr. Johnson. He lived at the end of my route and never tipped and was always yelling at me through his screen door if I missed his porch.

"Hey, you little idiot. Stop throwing your papers on my lawn."

I did stop throwing the papers on his lawn. Instead, I started throwing them on his roof. He was quiet for my next few rounds, probably very satisfied with himself that he could cross the tedious chore of walking three steps from his porch off of his pathetic life list. By then there was a pile of papers on his roof, and he must have finally seen them, because the next time I came by he was waiting for me.

Just as I started up his driveway, I could see his fat body silhouetted behind the screen door. He started screaming and charged off the porch and into the grass. I threw one last paper on the roof and ran full speed down the street. Landing papers perfectly on porches the whole way. Shortly after, I had enough money to buy my bike. And I loved it.

I was out riding my new bike when an older boy stopped me and said he needed to borrow it. He promised to bring it right back. By then he had one hand on the handlebars, and up close he looked like a kid who loved to kick puppies. He had dirt on his face and on his jeans and sounded nasal when he cursed. He spit a lot. I knew this was wrong and didn't want to give it to him, but he looked at me like a wild jackal that had just cornered a bunny. It was either me or the bike. I felt helpless, watching as he took off at full speed, popping a wheelie as he went. I waited a little while and then burst into tears. I knew I would never see my bike again. Then I ran home to Dad.

At the speed of light he had me in the cab of the truck and we sped off in the last direction I had seen the bike. We went up and down every street in the neighborhood, but it started to get dark and we still hadn't found it. I was in tears thinking it was over, but Dad was determined. Nothing was going to rob his son of this joy. Just then we turned a corner and saw the kid gathered with some others. We raced to where they were and Dad slammed on the brakes and jumped out of the truck. I don't remember what he said, but I'm pretty sure that kid never stole anything again. Driving home, passersby would have seen a working-class guy driving a beat-up pickup with his kid's bike in the back. I saw a hero.

All kids grow up in hopes of discovering their dad is secretly a superhero. I already had my hunches. It was in the way I could go after him with everything I had and know that he could take it. And more. Or the way he could slay the monsters in the closet without opening the door. Or the way the whole universe came to order the minute he strode through the door after a long day of fighting off the dragons.

It was with his strength that I first broke through the gravitational confinements of this world when he threw me in the air to experience the freedom of flying. From the heights of my launch I flew headfirst toward the ground with no fear, knowing he was waiting to catch me in his arms. In the tossing and tumbling on the carpet I began to understand the rules of the universe. That there is a threat in the limitations of my own strength. And a peace in the limitlessness of his. As I got bigger, my bravery grew in the shadows of his strength.

Once while playing I noticed a scar on his knee. It went from below his kneecap all the way to the top, and if I put my ear next to it could hear it grind and pop. He would sometimes say he was the bionic man. But I already knew that.

"Daddy, how did you get this scar?"

Dad had been one of the most successful guys at his high school, a champion athlete dating a popular cheerleader, and he still had the athletic build to prove it. He had a charisma and a drive that left no doubt for anybody lucky enough to know him that he was headed toward great things. His life's passion was baseball, and through years of dedication and determination he had become one of the best players his school had seen.

He was an all-star catcher and broke many of the high school batting records. This led to a professional recruitment opportunity his junior year, with several franchises expressing interest in him joining after graduation. It had always been his dream to play professional ball. If he could become a pro he would have achieved everything he hoped for, and life would go on happily ever after. Heading into his junior year of high school, this dream was on the verge of reality. He just had to stay healthy and post some good numbers in his final season.

For some reason he decided to play football that year. Being a natural athlete, it was easy enough for him to become a starter and an important part of the team. He played linebacker and in a big rivalry game found himself staring down a running back coming at him in full force. He made the stop but in the process his knee twisted in the wrong direction. I was told you could hear the pop from the stands. Then the scream. Before anybody knew to call an ambulance, Dad's father was on the field in the family station wagon, getting him to the hospital. Several surgeries later he would be able to walk and have a normal life, but the dream of playing professional baseball was gone.

"Daddy, does it still hurt?"

There was a deep pain in his eyes, but it wasn't from his knee.

During those years hospitals were using some experimental drugs as painkillers. They were very effective at numbing all physical pain but no one was quite sure of the side effects. The physical pain was great, more than anything Dad had experienced before. When he got out of the hospital and began rehabilitation on his knee, this medication became an important partner in the process. He pushed the physical limits of recovery, but with it came a pain so great that he needed help. The miracles of modern medicine came to the rescue to stand between him and the pain, and he would be forever in its debt.

But with this, another battle had begun—one that no one would see from the outside. I don't think he even knew. Though the physical wounds of his knee were healing, the emotional ones were beginning to grow. There seemed to be an inverse relationship between the two. He would recover quicker and better than the doctors expected, which gave him great hope that he would be able to play ball again. Maybe not as a catcher, but at least another position.

Hope produced courage. Courage produced strength. But strength produced pain. And with the pain came more painkillers. And on the back of the pills a shadow slipped, slowly creeping into his bloodstream, finding a way to his soul.

Hope is a dangerous weapon. If it's pure, those in which it rests will do great feats. But hope in anything less, no matter how slight at first, will ultimately lead to destruction. These painkillers gave my dad great hope that he could push to physical recovery and still achieve his lifelong dream. He would get close. But his body would never heal enough for him to play professional baseball. The physical pain of getting 90 percent of the way toward his dream was nothing compared to the emotional pain of falling short of the last 10.

He had already learned how to numb his physical pain. It wouldn't be enough for the pain he now faced. He would need something stronger. Under that shadow, a menace grew. He began to doubt who he was, or forget entirely, and the menace gathered strength until in its full force it ultimately challenged the man who stood in its way. Eventually this menace became my other dad.

Summer was coming up, and I started bugging Dad again about the secret fishing hole. I was only ten years old and he said I wasn't ready to go there, but he would take me to another place he loved. It was called Angel Falls. There he would teach me how to fish a river. From the campsite we hiked a ways upstream until we found the hole he was looking for. There was a small cascade of water falling down several boulders into a deep pool.

A casting distance below was a tree, long ago fallen into the river and still shaded by the stand of ponderosas where it once stood. Its surface was worn smooth and was large enough for both of us to climb out on. The river flowed under and around the log, creating an undercut bank in the grass on the opposite shore. The water was clear, and between us and the cascade I could see dozens of small boulders—perfect hiding places for trout. Past us the river tumbled down another set of boulders, through the campground, and then made its way out of the mountains and into the San Joaquin valley below.

Dad was gentle and patient when we fished. Like he wanted to pass something along to me—an important part of himself found only near the river. We sat for hours talking about the need to be present and tuned in to the water in order to catch fish. We talked about where the water came from and where it was going, and about our place in the stream. He went on and on about being safe, about not falling in. He said the river was as dangerous as it was beautiful. Though the surface seemed calm, below it was an undercurrent powerful enough to sweep away even the strongest fisherman. If I were to fall, he said to get out quickly. Because in every river there is a point past which there is no way to survive.

It was years later I realized he wasn't talking about fishing.

We didn't catch any fish that day, but it felt like something important happened. Like maybe I grew a couple of inches. Or I became less innocent about the world. I got off the log and fished by myself from shore. After a while I looked around and noticed Dad was no longer there. I continued fishing, assuming he would be right back and got nervous when he wasn't. I began calling for him, and soon my calls turned to cries.

Heart pounding, I dropped my pole and rushed around the fishing hole but still didn't find him. I went to the last place I saw him, and when he wasn't there, panic set in. I thought maybe he fell in the water, so I ran up and down the river yelling for him. A heaviness descended on me and not knowing what to do, I began to walk downstream to where I thought our campsite was. When I finally made it to our site, he was sitting on the bench. He looked different. I was relieved to have found him, but the heaviness remained. It was a fear that someday I would search and he wouldn't be there.

We didn't talk much about fishing after this trip. A distance grew in his eyes, and he didn't notice me tugging on his shirtsleeve. I spent the rest of that summer playing catch by myself or swimming with my sister or riding my bike around on the quad at the high school. I would get there early, before the sun got too hot, and play until there was no place to escape the heat. Marking the main entrance was a concrete monument shaped like a crescent moon that stood a little taller than me. Before heading to the school quad, I liked to climb up and sit on the moon for a while. I would lean into the warmth of the crescent and, with one leg dangling off the side, imagine what universe I was going to escape to that day.

The entry to the high school was a breezeway tunnel opening into the heart of the campus. The quad had concrete walkways around the perimeter and cutting through the center, creating a patchwork of grass in the middle. I'm sure it was designed with the greatest efficiency in mind, taking into account how students and faculty could best get to and from their various classrooms with their heavy loads of books and papers. For me it was a personal BMX racetrack that began at the right of the entryway next to a long bench and a bank of pay phones. My favorite time to race was late summer. That's when the cheerleaders would practice.

Grandpa had recently built my sister and me some stilts out of a couple of wooden two-by-twos with blocks of scrap wood bolted to them. I had practiced on the stilts all summer and could now walk almost endlessly and even do some simple stunts, like climbing up stairs or walking backward. I had the blocks raised to their highest point, which was probably only a foot or two, but it felt like I was on top of the world. I liked the air way up there. The blocks were too high for me to start from the ground so I would stand on the bench next to the pay phones, and with one foot up on a block, steady the stilts before my ascent. I would come out of the tunnel as fast as I could and do a lap around the cheerleaders as they practiced.

A little boy on stilts has a similar effect to a cute guy pushing a baby stroller, and though I pretended to ignore them, I craved their attention. Since my only path seemed to circle them, I'm pretty sure they figured it out. During breaks from their practice they would call me over and take turns giggling as they tried to walk on the stilts. One of the cheerleaders asked me my name, and every morning when I came back she would call it out. She was a rainbow in the dark clouds gathering above me, and the sound of her voice in the morning got me through the rest of the summer. I never saw her again after school started, but I never forgot how it felt to have an angel call my name.

As time passed, Dad descended into his darker self. I came home after school one day and he was already sitting in his overstuffed brown recliner with the record player on. The drawer of his side table was open. My sister and I were told never to look in that drawer, but curiosity once got the better of me and I peeked in. There were some dangerous-looking tools inside. Like something a doctor would use, or maybe a scientist in a lab. I didn't know what they were, but knew they were from a world we weren't meant to visit, and they occasionally came to our world to kidnap my dad.

Fear set in and I jumped on my bike and rode away as quickly as I could. Past the end of the cul-de-sac, past the high school, and to the chain-link fence bordering the Sumps. I crawled through an opening in the fence and disappeared. I wasn't sure when I would go back. Maybe never.

Nightfall came and I knew Mom would be worried, so I made my way home. When I got there Dad was already gone. His body was there, but he was elsewhere. The first time this happened I thought maybe he was just hiding in his body, but when I climbed onto his lap to find him he wasn't there. His eyes were distant and didn't look like his. They were those of someone else. Of the kidnapper who took over Dad's body while he was away. I learned to just leave until he came back.

When he did return he was tired and bruised as if he had been running or fighting or both. If I could catch him before he fell asleep in his chair, he would sometimes still have the strength to play on the floor. Other times, when he didn't, he would just smile to let me know he was home. That was enough. I crawled onto his lap and he smiled. I was just glad he had come back.

But the distance always returned. It came first through his eyes and then his voice and then his touch. It was a barrier, but not a wall. I think a wall would have been easier to deal with over the long term. It would have been difficult at first, an onerous obstruction between a father and son. The constant knocking until my knuckles bled. But over time I could get used to it and decorate it with pretty pictures in hopes that one day they would become windows.

But the distance was different. It was a mirage in the desert that you desperately walk toward through the heat of the day, only to find that when you get to the place the water should be it's still as far as when you started. Only in my childhood, the mirage was a game of catch in the backyard. And hope was forever taunting on the horizon.

It takes a dangerously long time for someone who is fighting with drugs to accept the reality that they are in fact fighting. Drugs are a menace, grown in the shadows of an evil world to stealthily prey upon victims in ours. They come to steal and to kill and to destroy both their hosts and everybody they love, or who loves them. Their will is bent on the utter ruin of a human soul. Few who are ensnared by their lies ever completely recover. And those who do may live with the scars for the rest of this lifetime. Restoration is the only hope.

My dad fought this enemy his entire adult life. For long stretches it would seem as though he had won, but then the foe would find a new weakness to manipulate. It would come at him so hard, and from so many angles, it seemed as if Dad were fighting off an entire army. He fought bravely, and every time he was attacked and near defeat some new strength would arise from within to fight it back to the very borders of hell. It would seem a victory. But it would be a false victory. A Trojan horse. For on the other side of hope is a backdoor that stands defenseless. And with every near victory the enemy was able to penetrate further through this door until it finally gained enough power to make its final attack from within. A man separated from his soul will not stand.

Like all of us, Dad's life began with innocence and potential. To grow up and grow old. To love and be loved. To have kids and a hope and a future. He never wanted this fight, but it came to him. It came in a quiet moment of doubt disguised as rescue. It said there was another way, a downhill path to avoid the pain. Maybe for a while it was easier. Or maybe once he realized he made a wrong turn and started back to recovery, it came and said there was a shortcut. But it's only by going toward the pain that we ever get through it. In the end it was only a slight deviation from the course that led to the fall.

The last night in our home was the blackest. As the darkness grew, the menace came to kidnap Dad for good. It took over his body and was no longer content with the confines of the chair. It controlled him through anger and confusion. When Mom realized the new level of danger that had entered the house, she tried to call for help. In a rage, the menace ripped the phone from the wall, and she fled. She grabbed a couple of dimes and ran down the street, toward the high school. I knew where she was running.

The menace stumbled around a few moments trying to get a grip on what had happened, and once it did, it took after my mom. I don't know if it was to protect her or buy her some time, but the man inside my twelve-year-old body ran after them both. About halfway there I saw him in the street. I didn't know if he had found her, but he was heading back home. When he saw me his pace quickened. I ran as fast as I could back to my bedroom to hide under the blankets. There was silence. And a fear. First from the sound of the front door creaking open, then from heavy footsteps down the hall, followed by lighter ones behind them. My door burst open and I don't remember anything that happened after.

Only the screaming.

CHAPTER 5

rites of passage

WE WEREN'T ALLOWED TO SEE DAD FOR A WHILE. WE were told he needed some time away to get better. When you're a kid you don't really have a sense of how the world is supposed to be, so you just accept it the way it is. But I was starting to wonder. I knew something was wrong with Dad; and when something was wrong with me, fishing always made it better. So I figured the best thing for Dad would be for us to fish together. I thought maybe this would make him happy again.

I fixated on fishing. When I was supposed to be thinking about when the Pilgrims reached America, I was wondering how the fishing was at Plymouth Rock. I wrote a story about fishing for marlins and took it a step further, suggesting that the marlin and I became friends and talked with each other. My elementary school teacher thought the story was written well beyond my years and suggested I pursue writing. She should have suggested I pursue a counselor.

––––––

The lake at our cabin is always lowest through the winter. A big power company owns the dam, and the water level is regulated based on some formula of energy production and water needs for farmers below. Every year in preparation for the spring snowmelt, they let the lake down about thirty feet. This exposes all the areas I liked to fish, so I explored the weed beds and rock outcroppings and took meticulous notes on anyplace I thought fish would like to live. I even built some fish condos out of rocks, then stocked their pantries with salmon eggs so they would have something to eat when they moved in. This was my preparation for the spring snowmelt. I spent that winter drawing maps of where the fish would be when the water rose.

Dad spent that winter in the clinic.

They said this clinic was the best around and helped lots of people who had the same problems he did. We were allowed special visiting times, and while he was there we became friends with a famous country singer. I never knew anybody famous and liked to be around him because he made me laugh. He had a couple of brothers, and whenever I would visit, one of them looked after me and liked to take me out for pizza.

"Mr. Rudy, do you know what's wrong with my dad?"

"He is addicted to drugs."

"What's that mean?"

"It means that your dad tries really hard not to do something, but then does it anyway."

Over pizza he explained to me that drug addiction is a disease, like the chicken pox, that could be treated and, over time, hopefully cured. He said the bad stuff that happened to me wasn't because of my dad, but was because of the drugs inside my dad. This made me feel better.

At first I was afraid of the clinic, but I came to love it. It felt safe, like nothing could take Dad away. Here Dad seemed like Dad again. His eyes were bright, his voice was strong, and he was singing. I had never seen my dad cry before, but he cried here. He cried when he told me he was sorry. He cried more when he said how much he loved me.

We talked about the new place Mom, my sister, and I were living and how it was close to the beach. We talked about my new school. We talked about fishing.

Spring brought with it great anticipation as the snow melted in the peaks, and rivers swelled and the lake began to rise. The mountains were awaking from the dormant winter, and hope sprung like wildflowers in my heart as it pushed through the cold snow to see sun once again. Dad would be out by summer, and because of all my preparation I had a new confidence about catching fish. I looked forward to proving to him I was ready for the secret fishing hole. I stockpiled fishing gear, organized my rusted blue tackle box, found a new lure, and then organized it all again. Each compartment hid away a different hope. Hope of catching a fish. Hope that Dad would finally be better. I organized it several more times just to be sure.

When summer finally arrived, I couldn't wait to share with Dad the map I drew of the lake bottom and show him the new fishing gear in my tackle box. He was out of the clinic now and in a place called a halfway house. I wasn't sure what that was, but it felt like he was halfway home, and that was as close as he had been in a while. Soon he would make it all the way.

It was time to go to the cabin and demonstrate my fishing skills. We got there early, and I fished all the places I had mapped. I caught a lot of fish. More than ever before. And I imagined how proud he would be when he saw them. When he got to the lake, it felt like Christmas. I couldn't wait for him to unwrap my nervous little heart and fill it with love and hope and courage and tell me everything would be okay. But when he finally arrived, the distance came with it. I fished alone. Staring in my tackle box at all the special lures and bait I saved for all winter, each compartment of hope was emptied until there was no more. He left early, and a few days later we followed.

After the separation and the heartache and the clinic and the hope and the halfway house, our family was put back together in a home near the counselors assigned to us by the clinic. It was our third move that year. Soon there would be another. Walking through the front door, we found him in the living room. He was there but not there, completely given over to the demons that had chased him his entire adult life. The mountain of a man I had known now lay unconscious on the floor, completely crumbled, exhausted from the fight and crushed under the weight of his disease. He looked smaller than me.

I fell into the swift current of the river, and he wasn't there to pull me out. The water got deeper, and I reached upstream, my little hand desperately stretching toward his. For a moment our eyes connected, and I thought I saw him reaching back. But he couldn't fight the current, and the water from the river filled his eyes. Then his soul. Already drowning, he could only watch as I drifted headfirst toward the falls.

We left with as much as could fit in the car, and my heart began its hibernation into an endless winter. A few weeks later I saw him in a mediated good-bye. He would now be alone. The counselor tried her best to explain to a couple of children why they couldn't see their daddy anymore and tried to get us to talk about how we felt. As an adult I still can't describe how I feel, and as a child I felt I was just dropped into the Alaskan wilderness with only a pocketknife to fight off the grizzly bears.

At the end of the session my dad walked out one door and we walked out another. I found him alone in the parking lot and ran to him hoping to tell him how much I loved him and that he was still my hero and he was strong enough to fight this disease and that someday we could still be together. And that I would be waiting. None of that came out. I just cried. In the darkness and the silence he said good-bye.

We moved again and I started school at a new junior high. Started a new life. The days turned to gray. That fall I got pulled out of school early, and when I got home my grandma was there, clutching a Bible. She needed something to steady her as she told me I would never see Dad again. He was dead.

A lot of thoughts go through the mind of a child when he finds out his dad just died. One I remember most was the realization that he would never take me to the secret fishing hole, and there was no way I could find it alone. Then I stopped thinking about fishing.

I didn't have any friends the day my dad died. The world is a difficult place for a thirteen-year-old boy with no friends. Especially when experiencing the weight of the world's collapse, with nobody to help carry the load. With the exception of my sister, I felt totally alone. Alone on my bike. Alone in the park. Alone in my thoughts. Alone.

At the funeral, everybody seemed to know what they were doing. When to stand. When to sit. How to say, "He's in a better place now." How to sound like they meant it. It seemed like a school play where everybody else knew their part but I forgot my lines. They were supposed to be simple. Just "Yes, sir," "No, ma'am," and "Thank you."

People would come up and say, "Your dad was a great guy. We are all going to miss him" and then stare at me, waiting for my line, growing increasingly uncomfortable with my silence. I would look at them and wish I could kick them in the shins. Instead I said nothing. Afraid to mess up the show, I just avoided the stage and looked for a place to hide.

"You look a lot like your dad," I heard from behind me.

I had been trying to not look at my dad, but his presence was impossible to avoid. He was in front of the room, lying with his eyes closed. He was there but not there. It looked like he was asleep at a fancy party. Like he found a comfortable box to climb in, to hide away from the crowd, and with the white noise in the background quietly fell asleep in his best suit. When I went up to touch him and say good-bye, I expected him to wake up, maybe a little bruised but not defeated. I thought he might ask if I wanted to go out back and play catch. He didn't.

I looked around for my own box to crawl into. To hide away and dream about places I would rather be. Away from this room, away from what life had become. When I couldn't find a box, my heart created its own. It folded the sides and bottom and checked to make sure all the edges were secure. I climbed in, closed the top, and sealed it from the inside. People could talk and shake hands and pinch the cheeks of the outside of the box, but they would never know what was hidden within.

A preacher stood up front and said things to make people feel better. He said a lot of nice things about Dad without ever looking at him. He talked about heaven and the river of life and about how Dad was finally at peace and how beautiful it was and that he was with God. He said that one day we would all see him again. I closed my eyes and tried as hard as I could to picture it all. I tried to see the river. I tried to see him in heaven with God. I tried until my eyes filled with tears. I couldn't see that far. They closed the box over his head, and I never saw him again.

———————

I've often been struck at the way different cultures celebrate a boy's transition into manhood. In the Jewish culture they celebrate a boy's coming of age with religious rituals and a big party when he turns thirteen. Native Americans would send their boys into the wilderness for acts of bravery.

At the age of thirteen, the rite of passage ending my childhood was burying my dad, and with him, my last hopes of being rescued by the hero hiding within the troubled man he had become. In the end, my hero lost. That was the day I stopped believing in heroes.

There's really no good time to be in junior high. It sits on the cross-roads of puberty and confusion and can be an awkward season for any kid. It's particularly bad for a boy who has no friends and whose dad just died. There is still the puberty and confusion, but added to it is a moat of emptiness keeping the world away, or keeping him away from the world. Days roll by like a slow-moving train through the desert. They are long, and other than a few moments of coolness in the morning, it's a desolate world of dust and wind. A full day could go by without a touch of life. Nothing much changed the next day. Or the day after that.

I went mostly unnoticed, which started off fine—but then it wasn't. Soon I realized the other kids had friends and were happy. I wanted to be happy too. There was one kid in particular who caught my attention. It was hard not to. He was taller than the others and was always smiling as he strode down the halls, head nodding to other kids as he passed out greetings wrapped in confidence and sincerity. He was as popular as I was invisible. The first thing I remember about him was his shirtsleeves. They were a little poofy. I was certainly no style expert, but his attire was questionable.

On a break between classes, I once saw a bunch of kids circled up yelling in the hallway, and in the middle were some poofy shirt-sleeves waving in the air. I ran over to see how this kid could fight. I shoved my way into the circle, and when I could finally see in, he was doing the windmill. Turns out he was a leader of the break-dance club. Again, questionable. But on the field he was one of the best athletes, and all the others looked up to him. That's where we first met.

"Hey. What's your name?"

"Roger. What's yours?"

"Tim."

In the classrooms and the hallways, I was an outsider. I had no idea how to fit in. I looked different than the other kids. In the constant moving and uncertainty of life so far I wasn't exactly on top of eighties' pop culture trends. My hair was parted the wrong way. My shirtsleeves were decidedly unpoofy. I didn't smile much.

My first day at the school, I was introduced in front of the class by my teacher. We had moved in the middle of my seventh-grade school year, so the classes were already set and the school was trying to find a way to get me adjusted to my new surroundings. The teacher was briefed on my background and was only trying to help. So she stood me in front of the class and said a few things about me. What I liked to do. What sports I liked to play. Then at the end she asked the kids if they had any questions.

A boy in the back raised his hand. I could tell he was a popular kid by the way he leaned back in his chair with his legs sticking out into the aisle from under his desk, as if that space belonged to him too.

"Yes, Billy, what's your question for Roger?"

"Are you a boy or a girl?"

Things were a little better on the sports fields. The locker rooms and lineups could be tough, and there was plenty of jeering, but the sports fields themselves were ultimately democratic. If you can play, you can stay. Fortunately I could play. Though it wasn't easy. If someone else had one guy trying to tackle him, I had three. It's just the way it was.

Our world isn't fair for the unknown. If the world didn't know my name, it could continue to have no consciousness of how it treated me. But somewhere in the midst of all that, Tim learned my name, and he was the only one who would use it. Every time he called it a little piece of happiness broke through like a star in a dark night. Soon I could see Orion. Shortly after, the North Star.

Then one day it happened. It may have been one of the most significant moments of my life. It was the first time I *really* talked with another kid.

"So, then. Where is your dad?"

"He's dead."

There was a pause.

"Oh. Want to come over and ride dirt bikes?"

Morning had arrived.

TWO

In Search of a Friend

*Friendship is unnecessary, like philosophy, like art. . . . It has
no survival value; rather it is one of those things which give
value to survival.*

—C. S. Lewis

CHAPTER 6

kmart hill

"Do you know how to break-dance?"

I thought it over for a minute. We were walking to Tim's house after school, trying to figure out who's good at what. Having already covered BMX racing, in which we'd clearly established my talent; and sports, of which we'd clearly established his; we were now moving on to other skills assessments. It was a junior high version of dogs sniffing butts.

In my mind I was a great break-dancer. I'd taken the moonwalk to its furthest planetary level and renamed it the Plutowalk. My King Tut had made me a modern Pharaoh. My popping skills were of urban legend, and my windmills so powerful, governments were applying for permits to generate wind electricity. Though I had yet to actually break-dance, I'd already agreed to be a part of Tim's breaking club. How hard could it be?

When we got to his house, he pulled a piece of scrap linoleum from the garage and dragged it into the backyard.

"The club is pretty serious," he told me. "They won't take anybody unless they're really good."

This had me a little nervous as I stood next to this piece of someone's former kitchen floor. The linoleum had a pattern to it with geometrical grooves that were supposed to mimic bricks or stones or something Italian. Or French. It's hard to tell, really; linoleum can be ambiguous. As I looked at the grooves, I realized it was possible they would interfere with the aerodynamics of my windmill. I also realized that like this linoleum, I was a fake. I'd never break-danced before. I had no skills. I thought King Tut came from Burger King. So I came clean and told Tim, but I think he already knew.

"That's okay. I'll teach you."

I sighed with relief and crawled onto the mat. I really wanted to be friends with him because I didn't have any others, and I was tired of walking through hallways alone. And since at this new school break dancing seemed to be a socially approved lifestyle pursuit, maybe if I could learn to break-dance, I could be a part of the club, and other friends would follow.

As I lay on the linoleum, he gave me some lessons about the windmill. I was supposed to swing my right leg around my head followed by my left, and then keeping my legs locked in a split position, tuck my shoulder, rotate my upper body, and then swing my left leg over in front of my right. If done properly the momentum would carry my body in large circles increasing in speed and velocity until body, legs, and arms were working in unison to create a perfect windmill.

He did a quick demonstration to show me how. Tim stood a head taller than the other kids our age, with a significant advantage of reach, though his arms and legs didn't have that awkward, lanky appearance of other tall kids. They were toned; and as he spun he had total control of his body. His legs reached almost to my face, and he used the strength of his arms to keep his torso in a disciplined position as the rest of his body spun. His body was a blur of dark hair and Converse high-tops. It was a perfect windmill.

Then it was my turn. I squirmed around the linoleum trying to find the right starting place, then took a deep breath and visualized myself as a windmill, gracefully spinning against a cloudless sky. I kicked my legs and twisted my body, and my arms began to flail, and I was flopping violently against the mat. Something was seriously wrong. I looked like a dying seal. I tried again, and it was worse. And I may have injured my spleen. From the mat I looked up to Tim and in that moment we both knew. I wouldn't be joining the break-dancing club. Which was disappointing, because I had already bought a breaker jacket.

———

Tim lived next to an empty field, across from a run-down Kmart shopping center. A developer purchased the property with great vision for the land, but areas once cleared for buildings were now covered with brush and weeds. Once a city dump, it was now a place where kids snuck through the fence to ride motorcycles or shoot BB guns or smoke cigarettes. The area was known as the Kmart hills. Trails rutted out with knobby tires surrounded the perimeter, and along them Tim and others shoveled mounds of dirt to jump as they raced through the hills on their Honda 125s and 250s.

Cops closely patrolled the area, and the rumor was that if you got caught they would confiscate your motorcycle and you might go to juvie. But Tim knew the best escape routes, and when he did get caught was somehow able to get out of trouble. His ability to get out of any fix eventually led to the nickname Kmart MacGyver, though no one had the guts to say it in front of him.

After the failed break-dancing lesson, we were putting the linoleum back in the garage, and I noticed all the four-wheeler quads and motorcycles. The entire garage was packed with them. The only space that didn't have something to ride was filled with tools to fix them.

"Are you a good motorcycle rider?" I asked.

This question may have been a mistake. In one complete motion he kick-started a bike while signaling for me to get on, and we headed off to the hill. I asked a series of questions as we approached the gap in the fence along the lines of, "Is this safe?" and "Is this legal?" and "Should we be doing this?" All reasonable questions, I thought. Questions, as it turned out, I would ask a lot over the years. He was pretty sure we weren't going to die, but beyond that wasn't making any promises.

I thought it might be a slow tour, but as we got through the fence, he twisted the throttle and headed to the upper part of the hill along the alley and backyards of neighbors aggravated by the noise. He was racing for the jumps. I was relieved as he passed the jump that soared twelve feet over a firebreak, then not so relieved when he headed straight for the double jumps. I wanted to tell him to stop but instead grabbed tight as I could under my seat and hoped for the best. I was a little shaken after. He seemed pleased with himself.

Tim was on a mission to help me fit in. I was born in this town but now felt like a foreigner. The other boys parted their hair on the side. Mine parted in the middle. They wore T-shirts with surf logos, and my shirts had buttons. My biggest fear at this new school was that I would stand out as different. At the last school I attended, I saw a kid get beat up for being different. Some eighth-grade boys surrounded him and took turns calling him a faggot. They pushed him to the ground and punched him until the teachers pulled them off. I didn't know why they called him that. Maybe because of how his hair parted.

I quickly learned from the limited graces of junior high students that it was a word reserved for anybody who was different—anybody who didn't fit in. I attended two junior highs and did orientation for a third. This was one thing I learned to be true everywhere. I didn't want to be a faggot.

Tim's house became the base camp of my transformation. It was a boxy, two-story house in faded tones of brown, and it had Christmas lights up almost year round. On the second floor were a couple of Juliet balconies where we once filmed a rendition of *Romeo and Juliet* for an English assignment so I wouldn't have to perform it in front of class. It was an older house but had a new room added off the kitchen that was used as his dad's bar. A few stools lined the front side of the bar, and on the walls behind were mirrors and shelves holding a large variety of liquor bottles.

We never hung out there when his parents were around, and if his dad was drinking we'd go straight up to Tim's room, but when they were gone we would sit at the bar. An anxiety hung heavy in the room. I could feel it and see it in how careful Tim was about handling his dad's things. The feeling was familiar, though I couldn't name it at the time. He was watching the clock and soon suggested we get out of there.

"Hey, have you been to the B-ramp?"

"No."

"Do you have a skateboard?"

"Yeah. It's rad."

"What kind is it?"

"It's a Santa Cruz. The one with the checkerboard bottom."

"Rad."

Awhile back my grandpa had found an old skateboard under his house and spent hours cleaning and repairing it so I would have something to skate the sidewalks out front. He even glued sandpaper to the top of my skateboard so my feet could grip the board. I would ride it until something broke, and he would fix it and I would ride some more until something else broke. The ride-break-fix cycle continued until the old skateboard was beyond the healing powers of Grandpa's woodshop. I'd saved some money to purchase a new board, so he drove me to a skateboard shop next to Baskin Robbins.

The walls were covered with posters of guys skating in empty pools and had a skateboard selection well beyond the thirty-one flavors next door. There were more than ten components to the skateboard I was purchasing. Each of those components required several additional choices of colors, designs, and quality of brands. Each choice in relationship to another resulted in so many decisions it paralyzed me in fear.

How could I possibly know how each decision would affect the outcome of my board? And from the start, how could I know what style of skateboarding I would end up doing? Would I be skating ramps? Downhill? Trick? Street? I could only have one board and had no idea how it would be used, now or in the future. Helplessly I looked to the guy behind the counter who, though a stranger to me then, I would have to trust to guide me through the decisions.

I started with the deck. From pictures in skateboarding magazines I knew exactly which one I wanted. It had a black-and-white checkerboard bottom with red caution stripes going through the checkers and deep wheel wells for extreme carving. Next came the grip tape with a design the shop owner came up with just for me. I watched closely as he put on the grip tape, rasping the edges with his screwdriver and cutting the excess with a razor blade. There was purpose in his movements.

He attached the risers and the trucks and the wheels and the bearings, pausing only to ask if I planned to do rail slides. Uncertain, I shrugged my shoulders. He promised I would learn in no time and added some black rails. He suggested a tail guard so when it felt like I was losing control I could step on the breaks, then a stubby nose guard to protect the board when it did get away.

Each small choice built on itself until a skateboard took shape. When fully formed those decisions could not be undone, at least without significant costs and in some cases, destruction to the board.

Unknown to me then, these choices would shape a part of my life with similar results. I had no choice in the fact that I was buying my first real skateboard with my grandpa instead of my dad. But I had a choice in what kind of board it would become. More importantly, I could choose where I would ride it.

Lastly the shop owner asked if I'd be riding over curbs or other obstacles. Confidently I said yes, so he attached a piece of hard plastic called a lapper to protect the bolt and axle of the back trucks from catching as it rode up curbs. Upon completion he handed me the skateboard and confirmed it was a good one. Before leaving he gave instructions for riding it, and with that, the courage as well.

Grandpa lived in the neighborhood below Ventura College and he knew of a good hill that went through the campus. As he drove me to the top, we discussed the route I would take and he pointed out the grass and ivy alongside the road that I could jump into if I lost control. I hesitated for a moment, then, looking at my board, regained confidence. Achieving high speed halfway down the hill, my new skateboard carried me through a secret passageway of freedom.

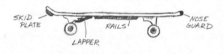

1980s SKATEBOARD

It felt like flying. I was above the world and the troubles it caused. From up here things were different. There were no limitations of gravity. From up here life looked beautiful again. Grandpa drove behind to clock my speed, and when we got to the bottom looked me in the eyes and said that was as fast as he'd ever seen a kid my age go.

Getting to the B-ramp with Tim required a hike to the bottom of a deep, wooded drainage ditch, locally known as the barranca, from where it was impossible to see the street, which was the idea. It was a nine-foot-tall half-pipe, and the skating surface of the ramp went "to vert," meaning the last several feet were completely vertical. This was designed so the good skaters could gain enough speed down one side of the ramp to get air above the other.

Once a year the city would come with a chainsaw and cut the ramp in half, hoping to dissuade kids from coming back. Every time the city did this, the locals who skated on it quickly repaired the ramp. It looked like it. The ramp was pieced together with whatever plywood and two-by-fours could be found.

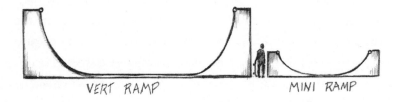

VERT RAMP   MINI RAMP

Hanging around the ramp were older guys wearing mustaches, some of them smoking weed, and younger kids who were pretending to be like the older guys only without mustaches. The kids hanging out nodded to Tim with approval, but they looked at me with the kind of suspicion that usually ended with a black eye.

"It's cool. He's with me."

———————

We have been created for relationships. Over centuries this has not changed. Extinction would come from complete isolation as individuals. Nations face the same fate: rogue countries, with fingers on the trigger, products of their isolation. In seclusion nothing good can grow. Loneliness is untilled soil with no place to spread roots. A seed dropped here has the potential to sprout, but on its own has little chance of survival.

A farmer rises before dawn, day after day, tilling the earth until the soil is ready. He then plants the seeds, carefully spaced in rows, far enough apart to bear their own fruit, but close enough to support each other in the bearing. They share the sun. They share the water. The closer they grow, the better they protect one another from the shifting winds.

I had been transplanted again, root-bound and withering. The uncertainty of where life would plant me next left me with buds on the vine; but without some tilled earth and a little water there would be no bloom. Then one day I was planted next to Tim, and my roots took hold. I grew stronger and life became more certain. Many factors played into this, but perhaps the strongest was that for the first time in my childhood I had a true friend. One I knew would be there when nothing else was.

For some species of plants cross-pollination produces the best fruit. By some mystery perhaps known only to the farmer, the combination of my past experiences with the new future to be created with Tim would produce a fruit unlike any around us.

We started spending more time at my house to escape the raw feelings at his, and soon days were changing with time going comfortably by. Tim found me near the lockers one day and asked if I'd come over after school. He said there was something he wanted to show me, but in the way he asked I could tell it wasn't because of the thing he wanted to show me. I knew his dad was home by the way he answered the door. He slowly opened it only wide enough that I had to enter by turning my body sideways, and we snuck quietly upstairs. In his room was a new drum set.

"When did you get this?"

"A couple of days ago. I had some money saved up and told my mom that if she paid for the rest of it I would work it off."

He played it for me until his dad yelled to knock the racket off and then we just sat and stared at it for a while. It was beautiful. The hardware had such a shine you could see your own reflection in the silver.

"You should get a guitar. Then we could start a band."

"That would be awesome."

We sat in the magnificent silence of a great idea. A few moments later we were bored again. We looked around for something to do. We couldn't make noise for fear of upsetting his dad, and we couldn't go downstairs. We were prisoners in his bedroom. There was a familiar darkness gathering in his house, and though I was too young at the time to know what to say, I decided to stay until it passed. He was a popular kid who seemed to have it all but who came home every day to a dark and lonely hole. I couldn't do life without my dad and he couldn't do life with his. He needed me as much as I needed him. We were a perfect fit.

"What do you wanna do?"

"I don't know. What do *you* wanna do?"

"I don't know."

"Let's go to the B-ramp."

"No. I don't like it there." I quickly added, "There's too many people and I can't ever get a good ride."

"So what should we do then?"

"We should build our own ramp."

I told Tim we could build a better ramp. He believed me. We decided to build our ramp on a corner of Kmart Hill, protected from view by surrounding trees and shrubs. It would be a four-foot-high by eight-foot-wide mini ramp. Nearby was a construction site where we found scraps of wood to build the frame. We made a few trips between the construction site and the ramp site and had a good pile of wood to start.

Tim snuck several hammers and some nails from his dad's tool shed, and we began construction. He knew exactly what to do and soon had a frame going for the deck. I marveled at how easy it was for him to pound a nail into the wood. He suggested I start hammering some wood together on the other side of the deck, so I grabbed a nail and took a whack at it. I missed. I took another swing and missed again. And again. And again. Tim looked up and motioned for me to stop.

"Let me show you something."

He walked over with a few nails and a hammer.

"This is how my dad showed me to do it. Tap it in a little bit to get started, and as you swing, focus on where the nail is entering the wood. Not the head. You have to focus on where you want it to go, not where it is."

Tim hammered a few more nails to make sure I understood. It took me awhile but I got the hang of it. We built one side of the ramp and spent the day riding down the wood and into the dirt. When we tired of skating, we sat atop the half-built mini ramp and from our shaded perch looked over a plot of land once discarded as a city dump, which was now bringing restoration to souls long buried in a landfill.

The following day we grabbed the hammers and nails and went to finish the ramp, only to find it smashed in pieces. Sometime in the night the ramp was torn apart. I stared at a ramp now in rubble with a feeling that we would build more, and that this would take us further than Kmart Hill. It would take a couple of decades for me to know how far.

CHAPTER 7

muy bueno. gracias.

A FEW YEARS AGO MY MOM GAVE ME A PHOTO BOOK THAT chronicled much of my life. On one page she created a timeline with school photos, marking the passage into each new grade. The pictures between eighth and ninth grades stopped me in my tracks. I was a completely different person. My smile in the ninth-grade photo looked like I meant it. In previous years I'm sure a child psychologist could pick my picture out of a school yearbook and say, "This kid's got problems." But in my freshman picture it was no longer visible. At least not on the surface.

Tim and I talked a lot about what we were looking forward to in high school. Academics didn't make the list. Occupying the place of anything sensible were sports and girls and bold predictions. To achieve such greatness, we knew there'd be sacrifices. Tim would have to give up break dancing. At least publicly. There would be occasions requiring him to bust out a windmill for the common good, but for the most part he would have to keep those skills undercover.

I would have to give up my Izods. Toward the end of junior high, I hatched a plan to break out of my awkward prison. It started with my wardrobe, getting rid of all button-up shirts and replacing them with surf shirts. This was followed immediately with parting my hair on the side. Doing it midstream of eighth grade would have called too much attention, so I made the transformation after eighth-grade graduation. I was expecting Tim to notice, but if he did, he didn't say anything about it.

I recently read an article about the most expensive residential real estate in the country. It identified the people who lived in these exclusive neighborhoods. It was a who's who list of movie stars, business moguls, and the children of industrialist families whose money seemed to beget more money faster than their self-condemning headlines. These are our nation's cool kids. Their moms don't have to work multiple jobs just to pay the rent.

While reading the article in my blue-collar Barnes and Noble, I'm embarrassed to admit how much time I spent wondering what it would be like to live in one of those places. Several of the listed neighborhoods are not far from where I live. We have the same weather. We have access to the same beaches. We get stuck in the same traffic. In light of these neighborhoods' existence, however, mine is no longer adequate. Their front windows look out to Bentleys and the homes of movie stars. Mine looks at a vacuum shop.

My quest for geographic significance started with the high school quad. Similar to every other high school in America, the social status lines were drawn in permanent ink around where you sat at lunch. Before you learned your locker code, you learned where the cool kids sat. Even if you didn't notice at first, one day, as if you stumbled around a blind corner onto Fifth Avenue, you noticed that things around you were different. And you couldn't afford to shop there.

Some kids would do anything to trade up their real estate for a more desired social identity. Each day over lunch they'd press their advantage. Some would betray friends. Some would give up their virginity. Others would pay with blood in locker-room fistfights. Just as the daily conquest began, it ended with the sound of a lunch bell. Then, as if on cue, the seagulls invaded to scatter everyone back to class.

Though my high school quest was less Shakespearean, it was no less calculated. I wanted to be cool and I wanted to belong. Being friends with Tim was a good start, but I wanted more. At the center of our quad was a concrete stage referred to as the Orange Peel. It looked nothing like an orange. Its official use was hosting important ceremonies such as graduation or rivalry-game announcements. Its unofficial use was hosting the cool kids for lunch.

A few steps across the lawn sat an equally significant area of concrete steps, and the two lunch locations were the opposite sides of Park Avenue, home to the seniors and athletic stars. The rest of the school could walk by and window-shop on their way to the cafeteria, but they couldn't touch the merchandise. The same steps wrapped around a concrete planter, and as they continued toward a maze of lockers became populated with other athletes and their girlfriends in descending order of class hierarchy the farther one got from the Orange Peel.

On the other side of a large grass lawn under the watchful eyes of the administration building sat the great middle class of high school. They happily went about their business, talking with friends and eating their lunches, keeping a careful eye for a vacancy on Park Avenue. On the fringes of the quad sat the niche players in their obvious locations. Student-government kids sat next to the student-government room. Drama kids hung out by the theater. And so forth.

I eventually found a home with those who didn't fit in any of those areas but somehow fit together. As if to fit our demographic profile, we sat on a short concrete block wall not attached to anything. It faced the quad but was a good ten yards beyond its official boundary. It was a crossroads of heavy traffic but not on the way to anywhere in particular. The wall was shaped like a squared-off horseshoe, stood about two cinderblocks high, and was standard issue faded pink. It was a perfect height to be either a chair or an elevated platform to watch the occasional high-speed chase by the administration or the awkward attempts at lunchtime entertainment.

Our association consisted of a loose coalition of soccer players, surfers, guys in rock bands (not to be confused with school band), skaters, and the undecideds. During the next four years I would spend most of my lunches on this wall. Because Tim was a star athlete and crossed several genres, he kept a main residence with us and had a vacation home in jock land. I had a pass to come visit whenever I wanted.

Tim and I coordinated the best we could on classes and were able to get several together, including Spanish. Language was a requirement, and a friend whose family came from Mexico also took the class with us. He'd help with our Spanish, ensuring an easy A. His name was Jesus, and he mostly taught us curse words. It seemed unfair for him to be there, like me taking English 101 as a second language, though because of a speech impediment it may have been.

I had a serious speech impediment as a kid. It was so bad that at times my mom was the only person who could understand anything I said. A Little League coach once pulled me aside in a game to ask what was wrong. I was trying to say that I was afraid something bad happened to my dad because he promised to be at the game, but I couldn't get the words to come out right and the coach just thought I was afraid of playing infield. So he took me out of the game and when Dad finally showed up he called me a sissy for not playing.

It took years of speech therapy for me to communicate in a way people could understand. Though it improved, I continued to struggle with speech well into high school and beyond. But I never got the kind of therapy that would work on the fear of not being understood.

Our teacher suggested we speak in Spanish as often as possible,

so Tim and I developed the habit of calling each other at night to practice.

"*Hola! Cómo estás?*"

"*Estoy bien, y usted?*"

"*Muy bueno. Gracias, me amigo muy loco.*"

"What did you call me?"

"I called you crazy."

"You smell like a *baño.*"

For some reason bathroom jokes were even better in Spanish, and inevitably language practice would end up in a contest of who remembered the most of Jesus' words. Once we exhausted names to call each other, we'd move on to other subjects.

"*Me gusta la* . . . How do you say *blonde* in español?"

"I don't know."

"Well, how do you say *hot* then?"

"*Caliente.*"

"*Me gusta la blonde chica. Esta muy caliente!*"

There was this girl. Her name was Amanda, and she was quite possibly the most beautiful girl in school. Or the universe. Tim grew up with her, which is the only way I could understand why his eyes didn't pop out of his head like a cartoon character every time she walked by.

"Rog, you should ask her out."

"No way, man. She'd never go out with me."

"How do you know?"

"She's way too popular. You're friends with her. Ask her if she'd ever go out with me. Tell her I'm *muy magnifico.*"

My image makeover hadn't progressed enough to ask out someone like Amanda. The outside was okay, but inside was still a stuttering mess. All I could think about were reasons she wouldn't go out with me. *I'm not smart enough. Not funny enough. Not cool enough.* My hair was finally parted the right way, but it wasn't the right length. My hair would be ready in a few months, but by then she'd be with some-one else. Things move fast in high school. Tim tried to reassure me. Throughout our friendship, his confidence stood in the gap of my doubt.

"Dude, you're awesome. Stop being a wuss and ask her out."

Barely into our freshman year Tim's romantic life was already at upper-classman levels. It was confident as a modern city. Boulevards planned to a master grid, self-assured and right angled. Mine was more of a windy country road, usually ending in a ditch. I started every Monday with the intention of talking with Amanda and ended every Friday with a pep talk about how next week would be better because I would wear a cooler T-shirt and my hair would look better and it might be sunnier so we could talk about what a nice day we were having and how we couldn't wait to get out of school and go to the beach. It wasn't that I lacked the courage to talk to her. The timing wasn't right.

She kept her hair simply. I preferred it that way. It was casual too. It could fall on one side of her face, framing her sea-green eyes, and without any fanfare she would adjust the tilt of her head, run her fingers through her hair, and it would fall down the other side just as beautifully. I watched other girls adjust their hair with great formality, needing any variety of clips and bands and the complete stopping of time to accomplish the task. Occasionally she'd wear her hair up or in a ponytail, but she usually wore it down, where even with a slight wave it fell to the middle of her back. It ranged from honey blonde to surfer blonde depending on the amount of time she spent at the beach. The color seemed to radiate from deep within, and on a foggy day it shone like sunlight. I was drawn into her orbit.

I became a stalker. Through careful observation I knew her most likely routes between classes. On days I was adorned with an especially fine T-shirt I would strategically place myself in the path of her travel, acting as inconspicuous as possible, maybe pretending to have a locker

near her class. The plan never seemed to go as well as it did in my head. Usually it went something more like this:

Sophomore: "That's not your locker."

Me: "Dude, shut up."

Amanda, walking by with a smile: "Hi."

Me: "___"

Sophomore: "Hi back."

Me: "___"

Then she was gone.

Sophomore: "How come you didn't say anything? She was looking right at you. Wow. She's hot."

Other days I would watch from a distance, imagining what it would be like to walk with her through the quad, the whole school seeing us in slow motion, rumors flying about how we were going out. I wondered what it would be like to talk with her. To hear my name in her voice. To hold her hand.

First love may be the most universal of high school experiences. It announces its arrival through aching in unknown chambers of the heart, doors unlocked by keys buried below the receding snows of a long-suffered winter. First love comes without warning and can leave just the same, though its memory will never pass. It lingers in dreams and hopeful near sightings. It's always near but out of reach, boarding a subway train, doors closing just before our arrival. There is nothing so painful, nor lonely, as the empty arms of unrequited love.

———

The only known cure for love is music. Also alcohol. I tried both in a variety of doses. Ultimately music worked best.

I thought the guy at the music store would get me. I thought he'd say, "I totally understand where you're coming from, man."

Instead he handed me a crappy Yamaha acoustic guitar. I couldn't get girls with this. This was a disaster. To match Tim's drum set I wanted a Fender electric guitar with an amp that went to eleven. The guitar salesman colluded with my grandma, who was paying for the guitar, and I got a Yamaha, though based on my clear need to write quality love songs they agreed to upgrade the purchase to a novice. I appreciated the sentiment.

I had a few lessons where I learned G, C, and D chords, and the songs began to flow. Tim cleared a practice area in his garage and set up his drums between the motorcycles and the washer and dryer. I didn't have an amp, so he rigged up some old speakers and a microphone so we could hear the guitar. He got behind his drums, and I found my perfect rock stance, and we stared at each other in disbel' that this moment had arrived. Before even the first stick cou' we both knew. We were rock stars.

There is a great ability of the male's imagination to see one's self completely outside of reality. It starts as boys when with a simple bandana we could be cowboys or bank robbers or ninjas. Even as grown men during Super Bowl halftime, when we lob a football to our drinking buddy huffing across the front yard to catch it—in that very moment, winded and worn out from a rigorous game of catch, we are the only ones in the neighborhood who can see ourselves as we truly are. Magnificent athletes, ready to be called into the big game should our services be required.

So in spite of the noise managing its way out of those speakers, we saw the full potential of our new band. There would be girls and arena shows and interviews in *Rolling Stone* and more girls, and we'd sell out the Ventura Theater and the greenroom backstage would be filled with our favorite chips and salsa. But it wasn't about that. It was about the music. Man.

Our band needed a name. We brainstormed several while sitting at the bar and under some influence came up with Common Indecency. It reflected our musical ability perfectly. Songwriting became therapy for me. It was a place for the pain. The songs were rooted in brokenness and anger, longing and disappointment. Tim understood because my songs resembled his own. With his rhythm they took on a greater meaning. Life, like music, was no longer an instrumental solo. It had a new layer, a context and depth. His rhythm gave me something to hang my songs onto and could bring me back to tempo when I got lost on a downbeat.

We played loud. He would start banging away and I would crank up my volume on the speakers and belt the lyrics. There was no way to hear anything above the noise, but in my head they sounded great. We saved some money to purchase a microphone. I was excited to get the mic set up and envisioned myself in front of a crowd, mesmerizing them with the power of my words. People would find such deep meaning in each line that their lives would be forever transformed. They probably would start a revolution. The *muy caliente* blonde *chica* would fall in love.

At the next practice we clipped the mic to the stand and plugged it in. Tim started banging away. I strummed some power chords, stepped up to the mic, closed my eyes, and launched into the lyrics. Tim immediately stopped drumming. He laid his sticks over the snare and leaned over his toms to tell me something.

"This isn't working."

"What do you mean?"

"Your singing *es muy horrendo.*"

Clearly we would need others.

———

Since I didn't have the courage to ask Amanda out, Tim set me up instead on a date with Amber. Her parents were gone, so the plan was that we'd all go out, and afterward Amber and I would end up at her house alone. She was pretty, and I was nervous, not knowing what to expect. I'd never been alone with a girl. I asked Tim to coach me. He said to be myself. Not helpful. Myself was in process.

While we were all together everything went great. It was fun and we were laughing and I was thinking about how cute Amber was and how I couldn't believe I was with her. But it went downhill quickly when we got to her house. I thought we'd sit in the living room but she led me to her bedroom instead, and I was expecting to kiss or something, but she just wanted to talk. Starting at an early age, boys get a lot of instruction about safe sex. For girls there should be an equivalent for talking. As soon as they get to first base with idle gossip they want to take the talking all the way home, skipping second and third bases entirely.

"Do you live with your mom and dad?"

"No, just my mom. And my sister."

"Where's your dad?"

"He's dead."

I could tell she was regretting her decision to talk, but it was too late to kiss. She crushed the vibe with her words. Backed into a communication corner, there was only one way out. The follow-up question.

"How'd he die?"

Here we were. My pants were being unbuttoned—still under the verbal metaphor only—and soon I would be naked. Against my better judgment, I let it out.

"He killed himself."

This was the first time I'd told anyone, and as the words escaped my lips, the weight of my past, the one I was trying to remake, came collapsing on me all at once. I turned into a stuttering, stammering fool and my words could not be understood. I stopped talking. She asked if I was okay but it was too late. I'd crawled back into my box and reshut the lid. I pulled up my verbal metaphor pants, got out as fast as I could, and walked home, crying in the dark. I never spoke with her again.

I laid low for the next few days, but Tim eventually found me and said he'd talked with Amber. Embarrassed, I apologized.

"Sorry about what happened the other night."

He wasn't fazed about the girl.

"Are you okay? You never told me how your dad died."

"Yeah, I'm cool."

"Let's jam later."

"Cool."

Instead of jamming we sat at the bar and talked about our dads. There's a certain kind of lost a boy feels in this world without a father. Tim felt it. I felt it. And we began to realize our only way out would be together.

CHAPTER 8

hobo jungle

WHEN SUMMER ROLLED AROUND I MET ANOTHER LOVE that got me through my girl issues. Surfing. The ocean had no requirements for me to be cool or talk about my past. I could come as I was, and every time I emerged from the water it felt like a fresh start. After Grandma rescued us from the fight at the beach when we first were friends, Tim and I began to hang out at a surf spot some called C Street, but was commonly referred to by locals as the Point.

The Point is the northernmost of Ventura beaches making up Pierpont Bay. It protrudes into the Pacific creating a long, right-hand point break with gentle waves crashing continually down the contours of its cobblestoned shoreline. At low tide on a good day, you could walk almost all the way to the break on an exposed run-off pipe covered in soft sea grass and moss. From there you could catch a wave at the top of the point, ride nearly a hundred yards into the cove, get out by the staircase connecting the sand to the boardwalk, walk back to the top, and do it again.

Every day that summer we'd get dropped off or ride bikes to the Point, and our numbers grew until there were dozens of parentless kids surfing and roaming the beach like a scene from *The Lord of the*

Flies. We were the pagan boys of summer, and that summer redeemed all summers before it.

There are several surf breaks near the Point, each with its own personality. The Cove, to the inside of the Point, is like an overstuffed sofa at your favorite aunt's house, soft and forgiving. Waves in the cove originate at the Point, where most of their power is spent. Above the Point, in front of some old animal stables at the county fairground, is a break aptly named Stables. In a stretch of right point breaks, it's a place you can catch a left-forming wave. Beyond Stables is a much faster point break called Pipes, where better surfers like to ride shorter boards, allowing them to do tricks requiring the speed Pipes waves generate.

RIGHT FORMING WAVES
AT THE POINT

Most of summer was spent surfing these spots, but one day we heard about a break even farther called Hobo Jungle that was seldom surfed. It got its name from the colony of homeless people who lived in the wooded area near the break. Around the grassy lawn it was just called Hobos, and other than the rumors of what went on in the woods, nobody knew much about it.

When we weren't surfing we were hanging out on a grassy lawn in front of the Point, bordered by a short concrete planter with a few trees in it. Under the shade, sitting on the planter, was a man named Bill. He would sit there all day staring over the water and over the kids hanging around the grass, never saying much. Nobody knew where he lived, and he never said, so I asked around until someone told me he was homeless. His eyes were gentle but carried a memory. He was the first to arrive every day and soon learned our names.

One day he volunteered to watch our stuff when the waves were better up at Stables. I was uneasy about it but everything seemed in its place when we got back, so soon we were asking him to watch our stuff as we surfed in the Cove or Stables or Pipes or afterward when we walked to the steak-and-hoagie place for a greasy bag of French fries. When we got back sometimes we would say thanks, and sometimes we wouldn't, but he would be there either way, sitting on the planter in the shade.

Tim and I decided one day to surf Hobos. To get there you had to walk past the nice boardwalk of the Point and Stables and with numbed feet pass Pipes along a coarse asphalt trail constantly reclaimed by the tides. Then you had to traverse the river and hike along dunes and wetlands to where a small grove of windswept Monterey pines receded into the ocean. At low tide several concrete gun turrets could be seen along the shore. During World War II, a Japanese submarine surfaced off the coast and these turrets were built to defend against attack. They gave a feeling of imminent danger to the break. From the beach you can look back to the foothills surrounding our town and on winter days see the snowcapped mountains beyond. It became our favorite place to surf that summer.

A trip to Hobos required provisional planning so we'd go in the afternoon after already surfing in the Cove and purchasing candy bars and sodas from the liquor store a couple of blocks away. Like

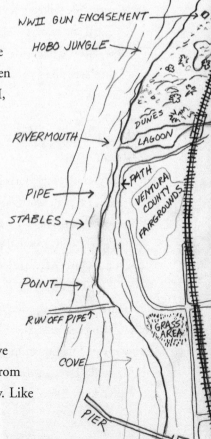

81

the summer, these afternoon walks were a transitional journey from our childhoods into future selves, one foot placed steadily in front of the other, shoulder to shoulder under golden sun. The ocean and river, sand dunes and foothills, provided a dramatic backdrop to a series of far-reaching conversations laying the foundation of our friendship, each beginning with an observation about the waves.

"Dude, the waves look awesome today."

Every conversation along the shoreline was backed by sounds of seabirds and crashing waves of the ocean. Summer was coming to a close, and it was time to think about our sophomore year. After a pause Tim changed the subject.

"Are you going to finally ask out Amanda?"

"I wish. We talked a few times though last semester."

"What'd she say?"

"She said she liked my T-shirt."

"I think she likes you."

"Serious?"

"Serious."

I let the thought sink in for a moment, then returned to the conversation.

"Are you playing football this year?"

"Yeah, I'll play again. You should play. You can try out at the end of summer."

"Maybe I will. My dad played football."

Our fathers are much closer to the surface than we think. I've found myself making random references to my father and have never been sure why. At the record store when the guy behind the counter said I picked a classic Led Zepplin album, I'd be sure to let him know my dad had the same one. Even now someone might say, "Cool beard," and I'll say in return, "My father had a beard," and the barista at Starbucks will look at me confused and say back, "$3.95 please."

These surf sessions with Tim became a safe place to talk of such things. The ocean has no memory of my past.

"Do you think you'll be like your dad when you grow up?"

In some ways I hoped I would. He was a great athlete. He was a musician and loved to fish. But I didn't get to know those parts of him well enough to know if they offset the ones I did.

"I don't know."

Between the words a wave emerged. It gave of itself completely. Heaving from an overflowed cup, rising and falling and returning to the ocean. We watched as if a gift unwrapped, after the silence returning to the moment.

I'm not sure how it came up but eventually Tim asked, "Do you believe in God?"

Tim grew up Catholic, and I knew he believed in God, but when his parents stopped making him go to church, he quit going. He didn't get it. I went with him a few times and didn't get it either. I grew up believing in God and prayed earnestly for my dad to get better. I even believed the power of my prayers would save him. When he died in spite of my efforts to convince God otherwise, I eventually stopped praying. It's hard to trust a God who doesn't look after little kids.

"I don't know."

––––––––––

In those days surfing still had an edge to it. Spots were heavily localized, and it wasn't uncommon for a simple drop-in at a new beach to result in a bloodied nose from a surfer who didn't think you belonged there. Though the Point wasn't considered to be a localized break, places nearby were, and those surfers would end up at the Point when their breaks weren't working. I was catching waves in front of our grassy perch when I heard an angry voice from behind.

"Hey, you little snake! Why'd you take my wave?"

I turned to see an older guy paddling quickly toward me. He accused me of taking his wave and looked determined to fight. I tried to say I didn't see him, which only seemed to make him angrier. I made a break for shore and could tell by the closeness of his cussing that he was right behind me. He nearly caught up to me as I scrambled up the beach and saw Bill. I got safely behind him.

I don't know what all Bill has seen through watches of the night, but I know that the other guy saw it reflected in his eyes and immediately knew what would happen to him if he laid a hand on any of the kids under Bill's watch. After his encounter with Bill the stranger ran down the boardwalk to get in his car and leave. Tim and an angry mob of kids chased behind him to ensure he never came back. For the rest of the summer Bill sat under the shade tree every day until the last kid was safely picked up by their parents.

I suspect all guardian angels are homeless.

———

I was settling into a new normal. That summer I would sit in the water and ask God about Dad and the world and watch these questions sink unanswered into the Pacific, where they were gathered with all unanswered questions and given back in the form of perfect waves. After a short paddle through the shore break, Tim and I would surf the last swells of summer and in the fading light of day talk about fathers and God and girls and the men we were trying to become.

Over the horizon wave after wave would rise up in a thoughtful pattern, symmetry suggesting an order and purpose, and the longer I remained at the water's edge looking out, the more I believed it.

Soon the swells would come in different forms.

CHAPTER 9

gangs and God

IN 1988 THE MOVIE *COLORS* CAME OUT, AND GANGS became trendy, like sushi or the color pink. There was rumor of a new gang starting at our high school, which had me wondering where I could sign up and if there would be matching outfits. It was confirmed when Tim and I were on a mission to crash a party with some friends and witnessed a "jumping in" of a gang member.

The party was on a cul-de-sac of a quiet suburban housing tract in the foothills of Ventura. When we arrived there was a group of kids hanging out under the street lamp. Some wore flannel shirts, buttoned to the top like Grandma used to make them do for church. They all wore hats, some backward, some forward, brims slung low, just above their eyes.

We knew something exciting was happening because a circle formed as if someone in the sandbox suddenly exclaimed he found a buried treasure. I wedged in to watch. The one getting jumped into the gang was a kid I recognized from math class. His name was Erik, and he wasn't great at math, but he was a star on the cross-country team. On my way home from school I always saw him running ahead of a group of kids with their shirts off; they were using them to wipe the excessive sweat from their foreheads. It made me thankful I didn't have to run. He stood out from the pack, with red hair and freckles, and he was crazy skinny. This seemed useful for the cross-country team, but I couldn't see how it would help in gang life.

Opposite the circle from Erik were a few others from school, all equally untalented at math as evidenced by the disproportionate fighting equation at hand. They closed in on him, looking angry and confused, like someone dared them to kiss their sister. Calling the shots was a guy rumored to be the best fighter in school and leader of the gang. At first I thought Erik would make a break for it. He could easily outrun any of these guys, and because of his training he knew every bush and back street between here and school. But he wasn't running. He was going to take it like the Buena High cross-country star he was.

I'd been looking for a place to belong and started to raise my hand to join, but after the first punch lowered it quickly, pretending to have an itch in my ear. They threw Erik to the ground, and I got nervous. I knew from the movie what gangsters do to a new recruit once he hits the ground. The gang closed in on him and as the circle tightened things got edgy, as if we were disputing the claims of the buried treasure. The leader of the gang swaggered up for the branding blow but instead of delivering a punch pulled Erik from ground and delivered an announcement he was now officially in the gang. This fight was his initiation and with it he went from being an outsider to being in the gang. He belonged. He also got a free hat.

Kids came from the party to see the excitement, and I was reminded of the mission to crash the party. You could almost hear the theme song from *Colors* playing over the cul-de-sac as we returned toward the house, five kids wide with a new swagger. We walked in tight formation as if bound by the chains of a chain gang. Only our chains were a metaphor for the plight of upper-middle-class, suburban America searching for a soul in the eighties. Fortunately we had the lyrical stylings of the Beastie Boys and Will Smith to put our plight to beats.

The scene played out in slow motion with the guy on the end of the formation nervously looking over his shoulder as if we were getting away with something, thinking the adults were so afraid to come out they could only watch through the cracked mini blinds of kitchen windows. But the reason they watched wasn't fear. They thought it was cute.

Approaching the house where the party was, I could see Amanda through the window. After my last dating debacle I lost any remaining confidence to ask her out. Tim tried to convince me otherwise, but I didn't believe him. But since coolness masquerades as courage, I thought if she saw me at the party it would vastly increase the chances of her liking me. The only thing between the front lawn and our first date was the bouncer at the front door. He was the older brother of one of the guys inside and played football for some impressive-sounding college I had never heard of. Our plan was to distract and attack. Tim was the tallest and had the biggest mouth so he would start an argument to draw him out while I snuck behind to open a side door. The plan didn't work.

Emboldened with ganglike invincibility, I imagined the house on fire, Amanda yelling for me to rescue her, then ran at him with my best fireman-shoulder-shove. I think he played linebacker because all my forward momentum had been reversed and I was decisively tossed on the front lawn. Then into the street. And then over a car. Watching my low-top Converse shoes create a full eclipse of the streetlight, I was glad the house wasn't really on fire. Amanda would have burned to death.

The following week I watched from our short brick wall as Erik got oriented to his new lunchtime real estate, learning who to say "What's up" to and who to mad-dog. They had their own L-shaped wall. It was nice. It had a concrete top that made for comfortable sitting and provided a wider area in which to leave their trash. They were laughing and carrying on and seemed to be having fun, perhaps planning their next gang outing. They all had matching hats. I knew it.

By this time I'd achieved my earlier objectives. I had lots of friends and was considered cool. Yet I was convinced I was insufficient on my own and began to define myself by associations. *I'm Tim's friend. I play in a band. I crash parties.* When you're dissatisfied with who you are, there are no achievements great enough to convince yourself otherwise. I didn't know who I was and turned to the unpredictable approval of others. Life was shrinking. I wanted to belong to something bigger.

Tim's parents were gone so often that we moved band practice from the garage to the dining room. I also switched to playing bass so I could lock in more to Tim's beat, and we began the search for a singer and guitar player to complete our band. We tried several singers and tried cover songs from R.E.M. and Social Distortion. Many came and went, and without finding a fit we ended up more often at his dad's bar where Tim perfected the trick of adding water to bottles of alcohol so his dad wouldn't see the levels were down in the Crown Royal. Since the life of an alcoholic is a watered-down version of the real thing, his dad would never notice.

Practices became an excuse to drink. We practiced a lot. One of the guys we liked to practice with was Clint. Clint was one of the coolest guys at school and a constant magnet for fun and danger. But in spite of his reputation, he was also one of the most loyal friends I ever met. He would follow his friends into any depth of trouble, even though he was usually the one who created it.

Clint was a year older than us and somehow had the line on every party happening in town. More important, he knew every girl at every party, and for better or worse, they knew him. Clint became our party Sherpa, guiding us to the thinner air of higher peaks until our previous paths were hazy in the distance. The weekends were full of parties, and midweek was full of band practices. We drifted away from the music. We met more guys like us and were swept into the adolescent movement of fatherless angst. While with others I felt the safety of the herd, when separated, I sensed the approaching danger of a stronger predator. I was being hunted. I could feel the footsteps.

A new darkness closed in with the unrelenting objective of unfinished business. Every drink dug a hole deeper into my past. I quickly covered the holes with sand and straw to blend them into the surroundings. I left the thinly covered holes as traps, continually falling into self-dug pits of unresolved pain. I scratched and clawed my way out of one only to fall into another.

I followed familiar ruts deep into a murky fear until, from childhood memories of my father, I recognized the path I was on. I looked forward and backward, and couldn't see any way off. The footsteps were closing in, and as I ran, I heard the cracks of twigs, felt the unsure footing of shifting sand, and felt the sensation of falling. When I came to, I looked into the mirror and saw my father's bloodshot eyes staring back at me.

I wanted to quit, to climb out of the hole, but the walls were lined with the slippery lies I believed about myself. There was no way out. This pit was dug with the unnatural tools of a darker world.

Out of frustration or avoidance or something worse, Tim and I began skipping practice entirely and going straight to the bar where inevitably the topic of our dads came up. Tim's relationship with his was unpredictable. His dad had bought a used car lot and his drinking got worse. If a day passed and he didn't sell a car, he'd get drunk out of depression. If he did sell a car he'd get drunk to celebrate. Either way, the drunkenness led to anger, and the level of danger in the house was rapidly increasing.

One evening Tim's sister was with a friend listening to music downstairs when his dad decided to wrestle with her. The wrestling quickly escalated and soon he had her pinned to the floor, punching her repeatedly in the chest. He thought it was a game, but wouldn't get off in spite of her screaming. The shocked friend watched helplessly, then ran to get Tim. Tim rushed downstairs to rescue his sister and tackled his dad at full speed, watching as his dad hit the floor, rolled over, and didn't move. Tim quickly got the girls safely upstairs and when he came back to check on his dad found him passed out on the floor.

With others we rarely ever talked of our dads. If Tim did, he never had a bad word to say about his. Like many men, his dad was caught between what he wanted for himself and his family and what he had become. Alcohol was a temporary solution. In time it flowed through blood and soul, and the contents of a man were slowly replaced by shallow promises of a bottle.

Somehow Tim saw through this. He saw through the mess and the anger. He saw who his dad was capable of being. Tim was hurt and embarrassed by his actions, but more than that, disappointed his father didn't see himself the same way. Tim knew his father. He held on to a hope I had long abandoned.

When Tim got his driver's license, his dad invited him out to the car lot. He had learned to expect the worst and was surprised to see his dad in a good mood. Drunk, but happy. His dad took him out to a line of cars and pointed to the best one.

"It's yours."

Tim stood amazed. It was a red Renault Alliance coupe with enough space to fit his drums or our surfboards.

Tim's birthday was a few weeks before mine, so I was still waiting to get my license. I got my permit through the local Sears, where in a linoleum-tiled back room adjacent to the automotive department, our hungover driving instructor turned off the fluorescent lights and slept in the back while we watched episodes of *Red Asphalt*. In spite of being told I'd be spending my first day of driving painting the side of the highway with blood from my dismembered body, I was quite excited to get my license. Until then I'd rely on Tim to pick me up.

It felt good to be in his Alliance.

"Where do you want to go?"

"Let's get burritos and go to the Cross."

"Sweet."

The Cross is a small park high above downtown with views of the streets and beaches of Ventura, and then beyond the Oxnard Plain to the Santa Monica mountains, which form the southern border of our fertile, half-circled valley where any hope could grow. It's a good place for perspective. It's also a good place for lunch. In Ventura, Mexican food is a religion, and when it comes to burritos there are two major denominations. Corrales and Johnny's.

Like most denominations, the core ingredients are the same, and things taste different only because of the spices. Still, we fight incessantly over which is best and define ourselves by the burrito we choose. I was born into Johnny's. For a time as a child I lived in the low-income neighborhood surrounding it, and since my grandparents and mother were members of the "church" of Johnny's, I joined without tasting others.

Tim was a recent convert. We ordered with the zeal of sectarian priests. I ordered a chicken three-way. Tim ordered a carne asada, but I didn't hold that against him. We grabbed a handful of freshly made flour tortilla chips in the large plastic bowl next to the pick-up window and headed up to the Cross. After eating he asked, "Are you ready for your driver's test?"

"Yeah. Shouldn't be a problem."

"Who's taking you?"

"I don't know."

"Let me know if you need a ride."

———————

As junior year wound down, I wasn't making the progress I'd hoped. I had lots of friends but still felt uncertain of myself. Amanda and I still hadn't dated. Tim and I still didn't have a band. We continued to write songs but none of them could break through the angst.

Even now, the distance between where I am and where I want to be never seems too close. It is an endless road with happiness visible, like shimmering pools of water on the asphalt, with the nose of the car pushing it ever distant to the horizon. Driving faster to catch it only results in burning up the engine.

By the end of junior year I had crossed every ocean of high school, followed every map and dug at every X. There was no gold. In its place were anger, doubt, and emptiness. Pain is a circle closing on itself, and since familiar antidotes are less potent, that summer I took them in deeper doses, doubling down, diving deeper and faster into the circle, spiraling toward collapse.

To make matters worse, I didn't see Tim much that summer. He was dating a girl who regularly went to church, and he seemed to be pulling away. He was trying to figure something out, a crossword puzzle with mysterious clues and interlocking answers. There was a change happening. Subtle, certain, yet guarded, in a way that few could see. He asked more questions of God and believed that God was there. I wanted to believe it, too, but my belief always fell short.

I was surprised when Clint told me he'd be going to a church summer camp and suggested I go with him. When he told me about the girls at camp I was no longer surprised. Chaperoning us would be a church volunteer I met through a friend who was living with him at the time. Though I'd never been to the church, I really liked him. Clint knew him a little better and also vouched for him.

The camp was on a small lake in the mountains and, as advertised, was filled with girls who were hot and holy. Early in the week I learned that God was a magic genie, giving anything we asked, which was awesome. I could use a God like this. Might be handy in a pinch. Later in the week I got the fine print. Twice a day we had to pay attention to a guy onstage giving a monologue about a Father we all had in heaven. I tried my best not to listen by thinking about free-time activities and the pot stashed in my bag. I had enough of fathers—whatever their realm—and the damage in my life caused by them.

The speaker wouldn't quit. He was a salesman, pointing out every feature and advantage against competitive offers. Before the hard sell we were offered a test drive.

"Go ahead and try talking with God this week."

At the end of the week we could decide if we wanted to drive him off the lot.

The days were filled with every camp cliché from every camp movie I'd ever seen, only more fun. The only place we were instructed not to go was the girls' cabin. We went there immediately. There must have been camp spies in the trees because we were busted on arrival. We had a nice little chat with the head camp counselor and the volunteer who agreed to watch over us misfits. Okay. Fine. No more trouble.

The next day we got into a water fight while boating on the lake. It quickly escalated until a third member of our flotilla ended it by hitting the other guy with an oar. We were sent back to the lead counselor and the church volunteer. We now had camp records.

The volunteer was an older guy who lived in my neighborhood.

He and his wife hosted weekly youth gatherings at his house. Somehow I ended up going to a couple of them with Clint. I'm pretty sure I knew why Clint was going. He was a genius.

There weren't any men in my life at the time, and I began showing up at this volunteer's house just to hang out. He was always cool to me and had no judgment or pretention about him. I liked him a lot. I even trusted him. He found something in me I didn't see in myself but wanted to accept as true. That week at camp he helped me find it. After the last camp infraction he pulled Clint and me aside and asked if we'd consider mellowing out. He suggested that we maybe even take the speaker up on his offer and try talking to God. I could tell something at camp had gotten hold of Clint, and he was encouraging me to do the same. Coming from these guys this felt genuine, so I did.

Starting a conversation with God can be a little awkward. I'd talked with brick walls with better results. I tried a few opening lines.

"Hey, God. Have you heard about my band?"

I think he'd heard about it but had seen better. Fair enough. I tried several other angles and wasn't getting any signals from the universe that God was interested in this conversation, so I moved on.

Night approached with a sadness I thought had been long stuffed into dark places and meant to be forgotten. I sat at a quiet spot on the lakeshore where childhood memories were triggered by the smell of pines and sound of jumping fish. Beyond the lake rose ridges of granite mountains, immovable as the feet of God. All of it—the mountains, the trees, the sky filled with fiery colors of sunset—it all reflected perfectly into the lake below, and I couldn't tell which was more real.

Suddenly the perfection of it all collided with the imperfection of it all. Tears long dammed fissured the rammed earth, and then eroded it completely. These tears became a tributary to the lake, joining thousands of others who've stood at the water's edge, asking why they've been left to ask these questions alone.

Everything at this elevation pointed upward. Mountains. Trees. As if they were clues to where the answers lay. I looked to the mountains. Then to the stars. Then to the lake. Finally, I looked up.

"Fine, God. You want to talk? Let's talk. You say that you love me. You know what? Screw you! There is no secret fishing hole!"

Now we had a conversation going.

"You take away my dad and tell me if I believe in you it's going to be okay? It's not okay. Is that how you show your love? Where were you when I cried for hours in the closet, asking you to come to my rescue? Where were you when I fished alone at the water's edge? Where were you?"

Every secret hurt was like a wild dog escaping from captivity. They manifested in accusations, originating from someplace deep within. They came faster than my mind could sort out.

"Where were you when my dad died? Where were you that day? You could have saved him. You didn't. I believed in you. I asked you to come and you didn't. Where were you? Why should I believe in you now?"

I fought with God late into the night. I threw every punch I knew how to throw, and he just took it. He took every childhood nightmare. He took every coming-of-age shame. He took every doubt of his own existence. Every resentment of it as well.

Finally, exhausted from the fighting, I just said, "You win. If you really want this life you can have it. You can have all the wondering who I really am. You can have all the pain that gets shuffled and restacked but never goes away. You can have all the inventions and smoke and mirrors I've created to hide the brokenness. If you want that, then you can have it. It's yours."

The universe seemed to say yes, so I emptied my darkness into the lake. In the distance a rainbow trout rose from the deep, leaping for the one thing it needed most, then returned with a slap of the water, ripples eventually making their way to the shore where I stood. Then all was silent.

When the hard sell came later that week at camp, I closed my eyes and raised my hand to ask God into my life. The pain felt exactly the same as before.

———————

At home the next week, I got into a fight on the beach and things seemed back to normal. Only they weren't. The anger was scratching off the surface to reveal the questions behind it. Why did God allow me to go through so much pain? And why did I need him to heal it? It was undeniable that something attached itself to me in the mountains. I could feel its presence. It could have been a new relationship with God, like they talked about at camp. Or it could have been a tick. It was too early to tell.

Tim and I reconnected at the end of summer, and he asked me how camp was. He was different. I told him that camp was fine, then changed the subject and told him about the fight and the girls. He kept asking me about camp. He was happier. I could tell he had something to say but didn't want to say it. He was dancing around it. I assumed it was the girl.

I wanted to tell him about my fistfight with God. I wanted to ask if he had the same questions, but something stopped me short and I continued the dance. I was embarrassed. I had spent a lot of time manufacturing a cool-guy image, and here I was with my best friend trying to sell him my coolness. More than that, I was afraid. Afraid of what he might think if I told him about what really happened. I was afraid God might come between us. I still wasn't sure about what had happened, but I couldn't deny that something shifted in my soul. Now I was confronted with something unexpected. Would following God mean losing Tim?

He then said something that changed everything. Forever. He said he found God that summer.

Great. Not that guy again. I found him, too, hiding in the mountains like some Unabomber.

He explained his experience, and though his was not in the mountains or a camp, it was a genuine encounter with God. I let go of the fears and told him what really happened to me. And I finally got to the main issue. I told him I struggled to believe in a God who allowed the things that happened in my life. Tim said he had the same questions. Maybe more.

In a moment of raw, teenage honesty, we broke down and through tears promised to pursue these questions together. Without each other, I'm not sure this faith would have lasted. These tears were our initiation to something bigger.

CHAPTER 10

as he likes it

To kick off our senior year of high school, Tim and I once again managed to get several classes together, including college prep English, in which with our friend Darryl we formed a reading group called Jorge and the Love Plumbers. Darryl was smart, had a penchant for mischief, and shared our love of a good time, even if it meant crossing the line a bit. The reading group was part of the curriculum. Naming it was extracurricular.

For some unexplainable reason our teacher took a liking to us and encouraged our creative pursuits. When she heard about our band, she was thrilled and asked what the name was. Our previous band name "Common Indecency" didn't reflect the sensibilities of our newly found faith, so we began working on more appropriate names. We ran several names by her but nothing was working, so we postponed the task until the point at which we would actually form a full band.

Through some new church connections, Tim heard Erik could sing and asked me what I thought of the idea.

"You mean Erik the gangster cross-country guy?"

"Yeah, I heard he sang at youth group."

"Seriously? Do they let gangsters sing at youth group?"

"He's not in the gang anymore."

"Will they let him play in a band?"

Tim knew Erik the same way all high school boys know each other, by what sports they play or whom they hang out with or who was rumored to be tougher than who. Tim sat behind Erik in history, but they didn't talk much. So to get Erik's attention he snuck behind him and flicked his Adam's apple.

"Ouch! Dude! What the heck?"

When Eric saw who was flicking him he got a little nervous. He'd heard about Tim, and this could have gone either way. Eric remained silent so Tim started the conversation.

"How's your singing voice?"

"Huh?"

"I heard you could sing. Is that true?"

"Uhhh . . . I guess."

"Want to sing in a real band?"

"Uhhh . . . sure?"

"Cool. Meet me and Rog at my house."

Eric agreed to sing with us, and he said his good friend Scott was a guitar player and could also join. For reasons far too numerous to list in this book, Scott is one of the finest guys I have ever known. The list starts with him having a half-pipe in his backyard. We met in Tim's garage for our first practice. It was mostly getting to know each other, but we could tell right away the chemistry was good and the band could finally become real. We agreed that in addition to writing songs to get girls, we also wanted to write songs about our faith. We just needed a name.

Faith can be fun when it's a new toy. Almost anything can be justified and you can say things like, "God really wants me to have a new bass," and anybody who argues with you is clearly an accomplice of the devil. If we were to write songs for the Lord, then I'd need a new bass. He has very discerning taste. I prayed for a few days and nothing showed up in the mail, so I asked Tim to help me get a job. He was working as a busboy at a favorite local Italian restaurant. I went in to visit and was immediately confronted with the black-and-white photo wall that seems to be a requirement of all legitimate Italian places. It was an intimidating collection of *la famiglia*, questioning the purpose of my visit, asking around to see if I was a good fella.

Tim was well loved by management and regulars, so when he suggested they hire his friend I began the following week. The money was good and helped to pay for my new bass, and between shifts at the restaurant and Tim's football practices we jammed with our new band as often as possible.

With a full band and gear we no longer fit in the dining room, so practices were back in the garage. Neighbors began complaining about the noise. Tim's mom offered the storage shed in back if Tim agreed to clean it out, so he recruited the rest of us to help. Erik was always early, as if he were avoiding being somewhere else, so they got started before Scott and I arrived. To get to the practice shed you could either walk out of the bar through the covered patio with a half-sunk jacuzzi that never seemed to work. Or you could walk through the side gate and along the fence until it opened up to the backyard, where the shed sat on the opposite corner.

Both ways had their obstacles. The shed was about the size of a one-car garage and filled from floor to ceiling with family memories, mementos, and his dad's half-finished projects.

"Hey, Tim, where should we put all this stuff?"

"Just throw it in the backyard."

Erik tried stacking things nicely along the backside of the shed, but Tim didn't seem to care, so when I arrived it looked like the shed had eaten some bad sushi and thrown up a mess of unsold yard-sale items. For months we would trip over and kick rusting items, fine-tuning a path on our way to practice.

The simple wood doors of the shed opened to the backyard, and the interior was a rough-framed structure composed of two-by-fours, plywood walls, and a tin roof. Erik worked at the hospital and was able to get foam egg-crate mattresses designed to increase the comfort of patients as they lay in bed, but which also worked to deaden sound. Some showed signs of where they'd been, so we tried to hang those in places we wouldn't accidentally lean against. To cover the plywood floor we found scraps of carpet in dumpsters behind carpet stores. For lighting we hung neon beer signs left from the original contents of the shed, and for wall decor we stapled Tim's handmade posters of upcoming shows.

To hide the old smell of aging wood and metal, and the new smells of used egg crates and carpet, we lit incense, which didn't erase any previous smells but rather mixed them all together so we sometimes had to practice with the doors open. Finally we arranged our instruments, amps, and drums, and there was enough room left for friends who swung by while we practiced. With some imagination and elbow grease the shed became our musical tree house—a launching point for adventure or a place of retreat when the adventure failed.

Like all good tree houses, the practice shed wasn't intended for girls. An adolescent version of a man cave, there were unspoken rules about this. But an idea surfaced about having a pretty blonde on stage at some of our shows. My inner rock star liked the idea of pretty blondes. That's part of why you start a band. But this changed when I realized that the pretty blonde would be my sister. Like all brother-sister relationships, ours vacillated between love and annoyance. But we shared a special bond and when she sang there was a power and a beauty that elevated the shed.

Finding where we belong sometimes catches us by surprise. We search for it in obvious places, but it's usually hiding behind humble doors, under some junk that needs to be cleared out. I'd spent a long time confused about where I fit, and after fruitless searching I found it in a transformed shed lit by the glow of neon beer signs, writing songs about a faith trying to make sense of it all.

———————

In English class our teacher was encouraging us to plan for college. She said in addition to taking courses like hers, colleges liked to see involvement in extracurricular activities. She suggested Tim and I consider one of the school clubs or running for student body government. Our friend Kevin, who had the sudden realization he wanted to go to college, had trouble making up his mind which club to join, so he and Tim decided to join all of them. At least long enough to have their pictures taken for the yearbook and prove their commitment to extracurricular activities. He asked if I wanted to join with them.

"I don't know. What clubs are you joining?"

He rattled off a list but one stuck out in particular.

"We're going to join the MEChA club."

"Seriously? Isn't that like a Chicano studies thing?"

"*Cómo?*"

Kevin was looking for a place to belong, and though MEChA club wasn't technically the right spot for him, being with Tim was. For a moment, with Tim he was one of the cool kids, lifted from an obscurity he feared slipping into.

MEChA wasn't my thing, so instead, Darryl and I began hosting a radio program broadcast through the campus PA system during lunch. To sell the idea, we told the administration it would be a cultural opportunity to introduce our fellow students to new music, while at the same time interviewing classmates and reminding the lunch crowd of important upcoming school events. We threw in that last part as a final concession in the negotiations.

The Rog&Darryl Show was going well until Tim was our special guest on what became known as the controversial Christmas special. Tim had the idea to make hats, similar to Native American head-bands, but instead of feathers in back there would be large candy canes. Attached to the candy canes was mistletoe. So on air, in between tracks of alternative Christmas music, we invited girls to come kiss our special guest. That was our last show.

After the failed radio show, Tim agreed with our English teacher and encouraged me to run for student body government. This normally would have been out of the question, but it meant getting out of fourth period and having access to those coveted blue "get-a-friend-out-of-class-for-important-school-activity" slips. I also heard Amanda was running for a position. I finally rallied the courage to talk with her, and she had incredible empathy that put me at ease in a way no one else did but Tim. I told her about my dad. I told her about my confusion. I told her about dreams I never told anyone else.

She listened. She smiled. She understood me. I wanted to spend as much time with her as possible, and being with her every day in fourth period was a good start. So I decided to run for student body government, though publicly I needed a platform to run on other than "Help me get a girlfriend."

The immediate problem I faced was possibly losing. This, of course, would ruin my plan of lounging around fourth period with Amanda, impressing her with my student body skills. It would also test the popularity I had finally achieved. These were coveted positions, and most student body government members were incumbents from previous years, already tied in with the special-interest groups of jocks and college-prep students and band geeks.

Brainstorming between songs in the practice shed, we came up with the idea of creating a new position so nobody else would know to run against me. I just had to convince the administration. In a stroke of brilliance, we decided to create a recycling department so if the administration said no we could spread a rumor that Buena High School hated earth. The administration agreed to add the recycling department to the ballot, and I handily won the election. Earth would have a new hero on the Buena High campus.

A big football game was coming up, and I needed to get out of work at the restaurant. Tim was a star player so he had a good excuse. After being turned down in response to every other option, I resorted to a fake ankle injury. The assistant manager was a little suspicious on the phone, so I had to come to the restaurant to sell it. I rigged up a fake cast and somehow got out of work, but *la famiglia* saw through the whole thing. They knew a phony when they saw one, and their black-and-white faces grimaced with scorn.

Our high school shared a football field with our cross-town rival. The stadium was named after a local Olympic track star and was carved into a hill surrounded by homes. From the top of the concrete bleachers you could see all the way to the ocean. Tim played defensive end and was already having a good game when the quarterback of the opposing team dropped back for a pass. Tim knew where the pass was going and got there before the receiver to make the interception and run it back for a touchdown.

The stadium erupted under the lights, and pictures of Tim emerged the following day in the local paper. Later in the game a player from the other team got into his face, and watching from the sidelines I knew by Tim's body language that was a big mistake. Surprisingly Tim didn't crush him. Instead he asked him, "Who's got six points, baby?" Like the rest of the stadium I was on my feet celebrating when I saw the assistant manager of the restaurant.

"Your ankle seems to be doing well."

I knew I wouldn't be going back to work.

Tim confronted me about the fake cast. He was let down by my dishonesty. At first I thought it was because I might get him in trouble, but it wasn't. That made it worse. I imagine it's what it might have felt like to be addressed by a disappointed father.

As football season wound down we were able to practice with the band several days a week, and we began focusing on our original material. A talent show was coming up with enough prize money to purchase a new PA system, so we began writing a song to enter. The process would usually begin with Scott and me coming up with some music ideas and running them by Tim. Inevitably he'd stop drumming and lay his drumsticks across his snare.

"This isn't working."

Next he and Scott would get into an argument about how often to repeat a verse before going to the chorus. Scott was usually right, but Tim wouldn't start drumming again until we agreed with him. Once we had a bed of music, we'd collaborate on lyric ideas. A line would emerge and each of us would add to it.

"What if at the end of that line it went . . ."

"Yeah, then we could say . . ."

"Dude. That's sweet!"

"I like it."

"Okay. One, two, three, four . . ."

Each of us contributed the best he had to offer, and with the sum total of our contributions the song became complete. In the process we became a band.

My first term as an elected school official started like that of most politicians, with me giving away enough stuff to ensure I would serve another term. The biggest kickback I had to offer were those blue hall passes. I'm sure that in previous years these passes were handled with great responsibility. I considered them earmarks and used them to ensure that my constituents continued their support of the recycling and girlfriend causes. Each day, a few minutes into fourth-period shop class, Tim's teacher would be asking, "So, where's Roger?" Just then I would come flashing a hall pass like an undercover agent badge, letting the room assistant know there were urgent student government matters demanding Tim's attention.

The first matter to present itself was a handstand competition. There was a debate between Tim and Ben, whose class was just across a short lawn, about who could do a handstand the longest. For the life of me I can't remember who won, but it was during one of these fourth-period interlopings that Tim came up with a band name. The name was derived from a Shakespeare play we had recently read in English class. Tim went through an elaborate setup and then pitched me the name.

"As He Likes It. What do you think?"

To help make the sell, he gave me a hand-drawn logo of the name so I could imagine it on a T-shirt. I was immediately sold. We ran it by our English teacher, and she agreed it was a great Shakespeare reference, adding a good twist of our faith by changing the "You" into "He." Erik loved it right away. And though Scott thought we could do better, he agreed it would work. Our band finally had a name.

One day Tim thought it would be fun to dress in seventies' garb and roller disco through the quad. He quickly had a number of friends onboard and plotted the entry on campus, the route through the halls, and how we would escape. Roller skates weren't allowed on campus so everyone was briefed on the stakes. The plan was to meet at Tim's house before school and hop in Harpo's Playhouse. This was the name of his dad's motor home.

It was old and beat up and awesome. It had faded brown stripes down the side, and the interior was done in the same color of brown. As a nod to its heritage the carpet had a bit of shag to it, and all the cabinets were that same Reagan-era brown veneer used in every office conference room built in that period, as if it were part of the larger strategy to win the Cold War. Harpo was a time warp on wheels.

We would park in the neighborhood across from the school and all come in from the northwest corner. Once we got to the quad, we would make a lap around the stage and head to the lockers. There everybody would break up and try to make it back to the motor home before getting caught. With the plan set everybody was excited and rocking out to the Doobie Brothers in the back of the Playhouse while I sat up front with Tim as he drove.

"Hey, Tim. I have a slight problem."

"What's that?"

"I don't know how to roller-skate."

He looked at me funny with a "How-does-anyone-get-to-be-your-age-without-learning-to-skate" look. At this point he was swerving all over the road, daring the guys in the back to try and stand on their skates as we drove. A natural multitasker, he answered my concern while at the same time slamming brakes, jumping lanes, and rocking the motor home.

"That's okay. Just hang on to my backpack."

I was skeptical at first. I'd seen him skate before, and he was really good. He could skate backward better than most could skate forward.

Later I teased him about it when he was hesitating to drop in a big ramp on his skateboard, saying he might be more comfortable in roller skates. I thought he might crush me for that comment. But he was convinced it would work, so I grabbed his backpack and let him drag me by the lockers and through halls until we finally made it back to safety. It's one of my favorite memories of high school. As I think about Tim, much of our lives went the same way.

The talent show competition finally arrived, and after months spent in the neon-lit practice shed, we were ready. The room filled with people, and with the people came energy. The energy was food, and we were hungry for it. We'd carefully thought through our first show outfits. Erik wore scrubs from the hospital, Scott donned a fur hat with earmuffs tied above his head, Tim wore a hand-drawn As He Likes It T-shirt, and I wore an especially fine uniform I got for working at Wendy's for a week. It was vertically striped in aqua and off-white with a matching aqua collar. Under it I wore the other As He Likes It shirt Tim made.

It was our first time onstage together, and it was the exact setting of every dream I ever had about playing in a band. The four of us backstage. A room full of people. Amanda in the audience. Our band name on flyers posted throughout town. For a moment my mind wandered from the room. I thought about singing with my dad. I thought about my first guitar. I thought about meeting Tim and how different my life had become. This was a new life.

Another band had already played, and they were pretty good. We would have to step it up if we wanted to win. We had spent countless hours rehearsing our song. We tweaked the timing, fine-tuned lyrics, and memorized every beat until it matched the rhythm of our breathing. It was just a talent show, but it felt like redemption to me.

Through the music and friendship with Tim, my life had

resurrected from the ashes, and a lifetime of hope was embedded in this one song. We were the next act, so Scott and I tuned up and Tim began running us through the timing and how he would count us in. The lights dimmed. The emcee announced our name, and the crowd went wild with cheering. We walked onstage as calmly as possible, looked at each other, and took a deep breath. Tim counted us off. "One, two, three, four." We launched into our song. Into our show. And into our future.

By the last note of the song I forgot about the crowd. I forgot about the loneliness. I forgot about every disappointment and hurt. I looked over to Erik and Scott. Then I looked back at Tim, and he just looked at me and we smiled. It was an unknown acknowledgment that the adventures were about to begin. We won the talent show.

The song was called, "Set Me Free."

CHAPTER 11

almost famous

It was a few days before graduation when I got the call.

"Rog!"

"Hey. What's up?"

"Tim's in jail. He's not going to graduate."

Tim and Clint were walking through the quad late at night to hang some prank posters and stumbled onto a freshly destructed stage and vandalized Orange Peel about the same time the cops did. Of course they looked guilty and as a matter of habit ran. They almost got away, except a backup unit was called and surrounded them. Surprisingly the cops didn't believe their innocence.

As though they had jailed the Godfather, the rest of us got to work determining who needed to be paid off, who needed to be bribed, and who needed to be taken out. We split up the tasks. I demonstrated my Christian faith by choosing the lesser of sins, barely colluding with others. Except as needed. But I prayed for forgiveness right after. I think there's a five-second rule . . .

Our English teacher went to bat for Tim, and after further investigation the administration realized Tim wasn't responsible. He was released to a curious group of friends who wanted to know what the showers were really like in jail.

Tim didn't have much to say about his experience behind bars. Hard time will change a man. In the days before graduation, we instead talked of plans for the summer and college after. I would attend Westmont with Scott in Santa Barbara, about thirty minutes away, so we could keep the band together. Other than music I had no idea what I wanted to do. As a result, I felt lost.

Tim decided to stay in Ventura where he could work and commute to a state school and get through college without any debt. He had a deep love for our hometown and didn't have any intention of leaving. Though he didn't have any idea what he was going to do either, he seemed less lost. A couple of days later we threw our graduation caps in the air and began a transition into a manhood nobody understood.

Autumn is an invention of college. Off campus it's fall. On campus it's autumn. In college during the months of autumn you can sit under a canopy of elms and through dappled light wonder about the world, knowing in four years you'll have the knowledge and enthusiasm to fix any of its deficiencies.

Scott and I shared a dorm room in Page Hall, which sounds much nicer than it is. Though it did have its own laundry room, and if you were lucky a freshman girl waiting for the machines may have folded your laundry because where she's from, that's the decent thing to do. If it was a guy waiting, your clothes would be piled nicely on a table. If it was a guy from our section they would be dumped on the floor.

I watched as new students got dropped off for their first semester. Mothers were crying about how their babies had grown up and fathers, who all looked like they stepped out of J. Crew catalogs, opened leather billfolds to pass out fresh twenties and hundreds like business cards. They seemed to wink as a signal between father and son that it was best if mother didn't know about this.

The first month of my freshman year was a big party until I failed my first test and realized I was no longer in high school. Talking with new dorm mates revealed they had all fared the same. We made commitments to study and go to the library and settle into college life. Down the hall one of the guys had a nice entertainment center, so when testosterone levels were high we watched movies like *Lethal Weapon 3*, knowing we'd all grow up to be like Danny Glover's character but wishing we could be more like Mel Gibson's. There's a scene in the movie where Danny Glover's character walks in on his son as he's shaving for the first time. In a fatherly moment, this tough-guy cop holds his son's hand with the razor and gently shows him how to shave. "Go with the grain," he says. I may be the only guy who's ever cried watching *Lethal Weapon*.

The nice thing about not having a dad is that you can create a composite dad from characters in movies. He could be both Danny Glover and Mel Gibson. For every mood or situation I could create a different dad, and he would always say the right thing and would never start a conversation with, "When I was your age." Inevitably, fathers of these new college friends would approach me in their button-downs and casual-Friday khakis to shake my hand and ask what my dad did for a living. In one question they could size up me and my whole family line. After an awkward moment I'd tell them.

"I don't have a dad."

But I knew my composite dad could take them out.

———

Shortly into the semester, Tim got a call from Mikee asking if we wanted to play the Melody Ballroom in Portland. Mikee was a good friend from high school we played music with and who starred in a school musical with Tim. He graduated a few years earlier and moved to Portland, where he was making a mark on the Northwest music scene. We'd never played in a ballroom before. Nor in Portland.

No one gave it a second thought that we lived near the bottom of California and Portland was near the top of Oregon and we'd be traveling nearly the entire length of our country's Pacific coastline to play a single show at a venue none of us had ever heard of. But to be fair, it was a ballroom. Tim did the driving math and determined that if we made only the necessary stops for refueling, we could leave after classes on Friday, play our thirty-minute set on Saturday, then drive through the night and make it back before classes on Monday.

Scott and I were packing gear when Brian walked in. Brian was as into music as we were and as a freshman was the best DJ on the campus radio. Hopping on a bunk, he asked, "When are you playing next?"

"This weekend."

"Cool. Where?"

"Portland."

"Oregon?"

"Yep."

"Can I come?"

The rest of the crew included a kid Tim was mentoring (against my suggestions he didn't have the time) and our friend Jeremy. Jeremy had taught me most of what I knew about music, and when he wasn't busy with his band would play with ours. In music and life, he's as generous a person as I've met.

While still in high school he stopped by my house after opening his first bank account when a guy from the power company walked up the driveway looking for my mom. She was at work struggling to support my sister and me, so I asked him what he needed. We were behind in our payments and he was there to shut the power off.

Jeremy asked how much was owed, got out his checkbook, and wrote a check to keep our power on. It was the first check he ever wrote.

Things at home were much worse with Tim's dad. He was seldom coming home, and when he did was so drunk and violent Tim had to regularly stand him down before something happened to his mother or sister. The following morning his dad was always kind and charming, as if nothing happened the night before. It was after one of those moments when Tim asked to use the motor home for the trip, promising it would come back better than it left. He took this responsibility seriously and lined us up for orientation. There was a special trick to everything, so Tim demonstrated how to light the burners and how to work the toilet. When he moved toward the table conversion, Scott was already in position,

"Got it."

He bent over to pull the table up but it wasn't budging. As Tim started over to show him the trick, Scott gave it a yank. The table came up with a piece of the floor still attached to it.

"Oops."

Nothing rattled Tim. Whether a major or minor infraction, he always responded with the same steady tone of one who knows how to fix anything.

"Great."

After lessons on the fridge stocked with peach nectar, our final instructions were on the engine located below the driver and passenger seats. It was old and not insulated and got hotter and louder as the trip progressed. The main thing to watch for was the oil light. If the oil light flashed, whoever was driving had to pull over immediately to add oil. He must have assumed we knew how because he never explained the procedure, though he did show us the emergency case of oil in an external compartment while once again stressing the importance of the oil light.

It was time to close the side door, take off, and leave the world behind.

"Hey, Tim. The side door won't shut."

Tim opened a drawer filled with bungee cords, rope, and duct tape. He grabbed a bungee cord and attached one end to the side door of the motor home and the other to the oven handle.

"There."

Now it was time.

The most freedom I've felt is on the road, miles from home, heading the opposite direction. The two-lane highway cut through a sea of orange trees and the treetops rolled and unfolded like green ocean swells, with the air as bright as fresh-squeezed orange juice. Perpendicular to the road, orchards were arranged in perfectly straight rows, one after the next like a series of long hallways. Watching each row pass created a rhythm as steady as a metronome. The California landscape, revealed in the golden sunlight, welcomed us into its promise.

Tim was driving and I was in the passenger's seat. The rest of the guys were in the rear lounge playing video games when we came at full speed to a railroad crossing.

Slam!

Tim yelled over the engine noise, "What was that?"

"The emergency oil."

Out the back window, Erik watched the case bounce down Highway 126.

"Great."

Erik came to the front lounge to hang with Tim and me for a while. After practicing and playing and traveling as much as we did, the band felt like brothers.

"How are things with Amanda?"

We dated on and off our senior year and continued to spend time together through the summer. She would pick me up in the mornings on her way to the beach, where we'd lie in warm sand talking about everything we'd ever done and everything we still hoped to do. One day she swam to where I was surfing. Just before she got to me she dove underwater and surfaced only inches away, her blonde hair wet and beautiful, perfectly shaped by the ocean, snug against the sun-kissed skin of her back. We floated for hours on my surfboard, letting our legs tangle underneath. When we kissed I felt something for her that was hard to explain. At the end of one of these days, she looked into some deep part of me I didn't know existed.

"I love you, Roger."

With these words my soul awakened. I wanted to tell her the same, but I never summoned the courage. Every day of summer I wanted to tell her. The aching built until the last moments before heading back to school. She held my hands and waited for my words. I could see myself reflected in the watery lenses of her eyes. The words almost came. They left my heart and on the way to my tongue tripped over a fear left from the last good-bye of my father. There was a sad silence in her smile.

"Good-bye."

I watched her drive into the setting sun of summer.

I replayed the scene every day after and when she returned on a school break, I told Tim I planned to finally tell her how I felt. I just hoped it wasn't too late.

Tim was into his fourth peach nectar and needed the bathroom. We were on a schedule and didn't have time to stop, so he told me to grab the wheel and jump in the driver seat when he got up. To save time, we were also supposed to sleep in shifts, but everybody was too excited to sleep so we just cranked up the radio and drove through the night.

Slam!

The bungee holding the side door came loose and now the door was pinned against the side of the motor home, held wide open by the force of the wind.

"Just leave it. We'll fix it when we stop."

If it had been an airplane, we would have been sucked out of the gaping hole. But instead the guys kept playing cards, watching cars pass between hands. We finally stopped for gas, and while we split up to get provisions Tim retied the door shut with multiple bungee cords and some rope. Before we left, Tim told us to buy some more oil and reminded us of the oil light.

We were in Northern California when the sun rose with all the colors of a new day. Crossing from front to back of the motor home required a game of Twister, but in spite of the air streaming in through the crack, the door remained shut. With cold mountain air blowing in we were freezing to death, so Jer lit the stovetop burners to create some heat, and on the next mountain curve the curtain blew over the burner and burst into flames. Tim continued at sixty-five miles an hour, yelling at Brian who ran for a fire extinguisher that wasn't included in the orientation (because you can't plan for everything).

Jer was near the sink and started splashing the burning curtains and Erik and Scott joined with the splashing and eventually the fire was contained. Tim's mentor kid was in back playing video games, and I was giving play-by-play action to Tim, who at this point was resigned to the fact that he may be working the rest of his life at his dad's car lot to pay for this trip. Brian ran to the kitchen with the fire extinguisher, tripping over ropes and bungees, and doused the already extinguished fire, just for good measure.

Tim turned the driving over to Jer and headed back to play video games. This section of I-5 follows the upper Sacramento river toward a summit along the highest elevation of the interstate. The motor home was as large as a duplex with a supercharged Dodge 440 engine. Like the rest of us, Jeremy had never driven a house before. An eighteen-wheeler was slowly climbing the grade in front of us and he went for a pass. He floored it, and Harpo lurched eagerly forward, but as soon as the cockpit cleared the truck the broad side of the motorhome was hit by a gust of wind.

"Oh crap."

"Oh crap!"

"Oh *crap!*"

There was a sound like the Titanic colliding with the iceberg. Next was a fierce sucking noise. It was the sound of air escaping through a new hole in the side of the motor home, created by the front bumper of the eighteen-wheeler. Tim, who was the closest to the collision point, watched the whole thing from the window.

There were shouts from the back in "this-is-so-awesome-but-it's-a-bummer-for-Tim" voices about what all could be seen through the new hole in the wall.

"Dude, I can see those yellow lines!"

"I can see Oregon!"

"Is that snow?"

Tim, who didn't share their enthusiasm, just let out, "Great."

Jer pulled off the interstate behind the eighteen-wheeler and after untying the bungees and ropes, our gang of teenage boys hyped up on candy, peach nectar, and video games spilled out of Harpo's Playhouse onto the snow in flip-flops and shorts. The trucker honked his horn, and outside of the window we could see an arm waving. It was big.

"Don't worry, Jer," Erik said. "We got your back."

I walked to the truck with Jer, and the first thing I noticed was a picture of a Tasmanian devil with crazed eyes, fangs, and arms looking like they just ripped someone's head off. Below were the words painted, "Don't mess with Taz." The door opened and out came Taz. I might have peed a little. Taz was a cross between an NFL lineman and an Eskimo bear wrestler, covered in tattoos and with more steel in his nose and ears than my first car. The Tasmanian devil on his truck was a self-portrait.

I looked over my shoulder, hoping Tim had learned how to handle guys like this while he was in the slammer. As I caught him and the others diving into the motor home for safety, I realized I hadn't noticed Harpo's customized license plate before. It said, "SunBuff." Taz was looking for whiskey and fighting and firearms and was instead handed a bouquet of handpicked wildflowers from a couple of music kids from California. He didn't kill us. But we all may still have recurring nightmares about him.

We found a Home Depot and Tim bought a piece of plastic corrugated roofing. He opened up the drawer to find some duct tape, and in true Kmart MacGyver fashion, fixed the hole carved from Taz's front bumper. Erik drove the last segment and was pulling into a 7-Eleven near Mikee's house.

Slam!

The top corner of the motor home collided with an overhanging pole.

"Great."

When we arrived at the Melody Ballroom for sound check, there were already people in line. The ballroom was in an industrial part of town, just a few blocks from the river. The neighborhood was gritty, with streets cutting coarsely through aged brick buildings, creating a maze of narrow passages and alleyways. Nirvana played here. So did Pearl Jam. It was the largest venue we'd been in as a band and walking through it Tim and I exchanged a look as if to say, "We made it." We felt famous. Then Mikee found us.

"What are you doing up here? You're playing in the basement."

We sound checked and set up to play for a small group of people who came to hear the bands after us. Erik stepped up to the mic.

"We're As He Likes It, and we're from Southern California."

There was a nervous clap in back, probably from a transplant, but mostly there was silence. I was a little nervous, but I looked back at Tim and saw that he was in the zone. He took control. He looked up, gave a stick count, and launched us into our opening song. I always thought Tim was a great drummer, but this night he was the best. He owned every beat, and his kick drum thundered through ballrooms and halls. He was our anchor.

As our confidence rose to meet his, we played tighter and harder than ever before. His head was down and sticks were pounding, and against his rhythm we rocked the basement of the Melody Ballroom in front of a cynical bunch of strangers, earning our right to be there. At the end of our set we packed our gear with the confidence of a point well proved. We loaded back into Harpo's Playhouse and headed south.

All boys measure manhood first by their fathers. Their stature. The skills they possess. What they do for a living. And like attractiveness or success, we ultimately measure by what we lack. Erik's definition was being able to work on an engine. His father was very skilled and particular with cars, and as a result Erik wasn't allowed to touch them. While friends were elbow deep in engine grease, Erik was only able to hold the light, and really wasn't needed for that since it was equipped with its own hanger. I'd long given up the pursuit of understanding an engine, for it made all the sense of a duck-billed platypus. But I still held a light to anything appearing manly with hopeful thinking I might become one by proximity.

Erik drove the first shift and had almost made it through Oregon when the oil light flashed on. Everyone was sound asleep so he pulled over to get the emergency case of oil. He opened up the hood and found where to pour the oil. Alone on a cold and rainy Oregon night, Erik finally felt the satisfaction he craved in his youth of working on an engine. Maybe he would be a man after all.

The motor home bumped its way back onto the interstate and jostled Tim awake.

"Why were we stopped?"

"The oil light flashed so I filled it back up with oil."

Erik had a new sense of accomplishment as he explained to Tim what had happened while everyone else was asleep.

"How much oil did you put in it?"

"All of it."

Tim told Erik to pull over immediately. He put in way too much oil and was going to destroy the engine. Erik could barely keep it together as he pulled over to the shoulder. The freeway noise was loud but all he heard was a lifetime of voices saying what an idiot he was for not knowing anything about engines. The exhaustion of the trip wore down his defenses and all his childhood issues started their way to the surface. What moments before had felt like a coming-of-age milestone now felt like one more failure, and he was bitter and angry and hurt.

Not knowing any of this, Tim calmly told him to get a light and he'd talk him through how to fix it. Erik crawled beneath the belly of the beast, and in the mud and the oil and the rain wrestled with the demons of his youth, Tim gently coaching along the way. Finally Tim called out to Erik, "Great job, man. You fixed it. I'm going back to bed."

Erik paused before climbing back into the cockpit. Along I-5, in the middle of the night, he stood alone in the rain, water washing the oil and mud from his hands and body. And with it, years of lies and self-doubt that he didn't have what it takes to become a man. This trip would be a turning point, a reference to look back on at various times of his life as a reminder that, in fact, he does.

Looking back, I realize that the trip may have been a reference point for each of us. For me it was the first realization that maybe the journey and the destination are the same. And if so, maybe who we travel with is as important as where we are headed. And maybe that's the same too.

The sun came up, and we were on the last leg home. The inside of the motor home looked like it had been on a yearlong rock tour of the United States. To get from the cockpit to the rear lounge meant braving an obstacle course of ropes, empty peach nectar cans, music equipment, trash, clothes, bungee cords, and half-passed-out guys. Nobody wanted to drive. The engine got so loud we stopped to buy earplugs and couldn't hear each other talk. Tim was wearing DJ-style headphones and took them off to yell through the noise.

"Hey, kid."

"What?"

"How old are you?"

"Sixteen."

"Want to drive?"

When we finally pulled in front of Tim's house, we were road weary and changed. Scott released the bungee and untied the ropes holding the side door closed. He couldn't open the door. Tim tried next but it wouldn't budge. Sometime in the night it sealed shut and now wouldn't open. In the rear lounge, Brian slid open a window and for a second was dangling halfway out before I saw his jeans and Converse shoes disappear entirely. Then heard a thud. We had arrived.

CHAPTER 12

ten mile creek

WE HAD A SHOW COMING UP AT A LOCAL BAR CALLED
Charlie's by the Sea. Charlie's was on the boardwalk next to the Point,
only steps from the sand, and from the bar you could look out the
windows and watch guys surfing into the Cove. The stage stood in
front of a wood-paneled wall, stained dark from grease and cigarette
smoke, and next to it were large windows where in earlier years our
underage friends could stand outside and watch us play. Favorite local
bands like The Mudheads, Something for Nothing, and Toad the Wet
Sprocket all played there, and when we were younger we'd sneak in by
carrying their instruments.

By now our band had played together for years, and a gig at
Charlie's was routine. After the Portland show we hoped for bigger
things to happen. A record deal. A tour. But so far it had all been local
gigs, and enthusiasm waned. Practice was showing it. Tim stopped
drumming, laid his sticks over the snare, and leaned over his toms.

"This isn't working."

I wasn't sure if he was talking about the song or the band. Then
he clarified.

"Do we even like this song?"

We'd been writing and playing nearly four years and songs were accumulating like boxes in the attic nobody wanted to throw out. There were more than thirty songs we continued to rehearse, continued to lug around from house to house and season to season, never asking if they should be kept. Our reasons for keeping them varied in sentimentality, but ultimately we kept them for fear of letting go. Each song represented a piece of the past—an experience, a lost love, a feeling we were afraid to lose. Onetime favorite songs became millstones around our necks.

Tim ripped off a piece of cardboard from a box nearby and listed each song. We'd only keep what made us better. In the dim neon light of our practice shed, we fought and kicked and cursed and ultimately let go of anything holding us back. This led to our best work.

College was flying by, and every break I waited for Amanda's return. Though she didn't come back, she would send me letters talking about college life and how exciting it was and how she missed me. I wrote letters back and finally got the courage to let her know how I really felt. I told her how I would think about her through the day and when night made an end of my waking thoughts she would occupy my dreams. I told her how much I longed for summer and for us to lie in the warm sand, like we once did, like I hoped to do forever. I told her every way she made me better. I told her I loved her. I waited for a return letter, and when it didn't come I passed the time by writing songs.

I found myself coming home more often to spend time with Tim. He was involved with a college group at church while also helping lead the high school ministry, and I would join him whenever I was in town. I noticed his sister was spending a lot more time with him. His dad's drinking got so bad Tim was afraid to leave his sister alone at the house. He asked the kids in the high school group to pray for his dad and continued to believe it would get better. Hope was hard for me but I too promised to pray.

His mother asked Tim to be home one night where he listened to his father screaming at her, on the verge of violence. His mom had decided to throw his dad out of the house and get a divorce, but he wasn't about to leave. Tim went upstairs to comfort his sister, but when they heard their dad chasing their mom, he rushed out and met her at the top of the staircase just as his mom was rushing up, trying to escape his father. He told her to go to her room where his sister was.

A second later his father was at the bottom of the stairs, stumbling his way up, eyes red with alcohol and anger. He yelled for Tim to move but Tim wasn't moving. As his dad got closer he continued to yell and Tim continued to hold his ground. His dad got close enough to physically touch him and paused, making a calculation. Tim was never rattled. He never raised his voice. He didn't act in anger. He just stood his ground and finally said, "Dad. It's over. You've had too much to drink and can sleep on the couch tonight, but you are gone first thing in the morning."

Tim's dad stopped moving forward. He stopped screaming. This was the first time he recognized Tim for the man he'd become. He knew he wasn't getting past Tim and he wouldn't be coming back.

College was winding down when I finally got the letter I was waiting for. I took it down to the beach and found a log that had drifted from forest to river to sea, now at its final resting place perched upon a dune near a meadow. I opened Amanda's letter, imagining it was her hand in mine as I looked at her face, beautiful in the sunset. She began the letter apologizing for how long it took to respond. She said she had something important to say and wanted to say it just right. I understood. After thanking me for my letters, she began.

"Roger, I don't know how to tell you this. I'm getting married."
And with that, the seasons of autumns were over.

———————

We decided to play one last show. With our most recent material we hoped for a record deal and though there were some leads, it never materialized. With college ending it seemed time to move on. Tim and I had been playing together almost since we met, and it was hard to believe it was coming to an end. It would be hard to let go.

The last show arrived without much fanfare. Only a handful of friends came to support us as we said good-bye to this thing we came to love. This band we hung so many hopes on, invested so much time in, traveled so many miles with. Tim gave us one last stick count, then one memory after another poured through our instruments. The death of a dream is a sad ballad from a talented band nobody has heard of. Our dream of a record deal, of crossing the country in our tour bus, and selling out the Ventura Theater, came to an end.

I lost my rhythm.

The band was over. Amanda was over. College was over. I spent the summer in Europe, trying to figure out what was next. Contemplative and confused, I tagged along with a cultural study coordinated by my philosophy teacher and quickly disappeared into the grottos and taverns of post-college Europe.

My teacher sought me out in Italy to ask what I hoped for the travels and gave some unsolicited advice. His theory of life was our souls are vessels that expand or contract based on what we fill them with. In this lifetime, he suggested, we should strive to fill them with things that are noble and true, excellent and praiseworthy. And as our souls fill, there would be more of us to offer. He went on to say at any point in life, the smallest adjustments to a current trajectory would have dramatic results over time. Perhaps when we might need it most.

To contemplate this theory, in Salzburg I bought a pipe at a tobacco shop older than our country. It was mostly out of vanity, because if I was going to contemplate anything, I wanted to look cool doing it. The shop was in a charming area of the city filled with narrow cobblestone streets and cafes and women meeting their favorite aunts for tea. Artisan shops lined the street, and after picking up some bread and cheese for lunch I came across a little shop filled with watches made by local craftsmen.

From a young age my grandfather has instructed me to be careful with my time; it's the only thing you can never make more of. Time is an asset, and how we invest it is ultimately how we'll be measured. Before this trip Tim and I talked about investing in a business together, not sure of what it could be. I'm not sure why, but staring in the window of the watch shop I thought of a surf clothing business. Tim was already designing band T-shirts and I had just completed a business degree. It would be perfect.

At the end of the trip I sat on a bench at the edge of a field, contemplating places I'd seen and looking awesome smoking my pipe. My philosophy teacher was sitting on the other end of the bench. He was probably stroking his beard. He asked about what I picked up from the travels. Cows were grazing in the field and he watched them as we spoke.

I told him about the watch shop and the new business I was going to launch and how successful I would be and how I was going to change the world. As we talked, he pointed to the cows. In parting wisdom he suggested I remember this moment and think about these cows and what I might learn from them. He got up, walked along the edge of the field, quietly, slowly, contemplating the cows. As I watched him disappear I wondered how he ever got to be a college professor.

Tim and I began brainstorming names for the clothing business, eventually landing on South Jetty Boardwear. Tim developed a logo and designed our first shirt. We were both working full time and between the two of us could afford to make a few shirts, but we would need an investment to get the company off the ground. Though we couldn't articulate it at the time, we began getting the sense there was a high call on our friendship. That there was something big we could only accomplish together.

We spent the following year saving money, working on designs, and volunteering with the high school ministry at the church. As summer approached I agreed to be a counselor at the same camp I once attended. Everything seemed to be moving the right direction. But I felt stuck. I was holding onto something—a piece of the past keeping me from the full promise of the future.

Tim and I were surfing Solimar Beach when I brought up a subject we never talked about. Solimar sits at the foot of the coastal mountain range, and in early months of the year the hills are covered with wild mustard flowers. From the water everything is blue and yellow and green and air delicious as salted spring. We surfed there often, in the purity of morning, before wind or crowds stirred the water.

"I've been thinking about my dad a lot lately and wondering if I should visit his gravesite."

Though it had been nearly ten years since my dad died, I'd never visited the site. I thought about it several times but quickly dropped the idea. I was afraid to go. Afraid of what I might find. Afraid of what I would have to confront if I did.

"I think you should do it."

I was hoping he would think it was a horrible idea. Then he offered, "Need me to go with you?"

Good friends give us courage to do things that are impossible on our own. I needed to make peace with my dad and put some closure to my childhood. Visiting the gravesite seemed a way to do this, and unless I told Tim I knew I'd never go. After encouraging me a little, he paddled into a wave to give me some space.

From vague recollections as a kid, and the occasional mention of the gravesite over the years, I knew generally where the cemetery was. It was at the far end of the valley, nestled at the base of the mountains. The valley is filled with farmland and connected by a patchwork of unmarked farm roads. It's funny how much bigger things seem in our childhood memories; following these farm roads I was surprised how quickly I arrived. I was hoping for more time to get my thoughts together.

My dad's death was never really mentioned and over time it almost became unspeakable. The silence led to confusion and ultimately guilt. I would feel guilty if I thought about him. And I would feel guilty if I didn't. The guilt was compounded by silence and the only comfort I found was in my sister's eyes. Because even if we didn't mention it, I knew she understood.

I parked at a building near the entry, and as I walked to it I was flooded with memory. This is where I last saw Dad. The doors were unlocked, so I walked in and sat on the same bench I sat as a thirteen-year-old boy, and the room was filled with voices. The voice of the preacher talking about heaven. My grandma thanking everybody who took time out of their busy schedules to come. My dad's childhood friend saying how much I looked like him.

I wondered if I did. From the bench I stared to where I last saw him and tried to remember what he looked like. I wanted to compare myself to him. To see if I was his size. To see if maybe in his absence I had grown into a man. I could remember what it felt like to be in the strength of his arms or to be called home by his voice, but I couldn't see him. And the questions remained unanswered.

An older gentleman who worked at the cemetery entered the room. "Do you need any help?"

The question was casual, as if maybe I hadn't found the right size.

"I'm looking for my dad."

Every day he sees someone like me, lost in the gravesite, looking for a father. He answered as if to acknowledge the obvious. We all are.

He asked for his name, looked up his location, stepped outside and pointed.

"He's up there. Beneath that tree."

I began to walk. I tried to feel something. I felt empty. I slowed my pace hoping something would come. Nothing came. My dad was where he said he was. His gravesite had some fresh flowers and a plaque with his name on it. I hadn't seen his name in a long time. I read it out loud: "Paul Thompson."

I sat down on that patch of grass and waited for words. Still nothing. There was tension in the time. The shade of the tree was moving like a sundial, measuring moments in hours. The sun was dipping lower on the horizon and would soon be gone. The only thing working was my mind. Memories were in motion faster than I could capture them, blurring any thought threatening to become a word.

I began to think this had been a mistake. Maybe I was wrong to come. But deep down I knew there were things to say. I just didn't know where to start. I was a boy again, tugging at the shirtsleeves of a father, desperately seeking his attention but having no idea what I would say once I had it. Finally a few words found their way to my lips. Words I hadn't said in a long time. They sounded strange coming from my grown-up voice.

"Hi, Dad."

With that my heart opened. More words came, and in them was a sadness, between them a silence, and beyond them a hope that the preacher was right. That someday I might again see him. And that someday I might look like him. The sun set, like the closing of a book.

The next time I saw Tim I told him I'd visited my dad.

He smiled, satisfied with the news.

"What did you tell him?"

Over the course of our friendship Tim and I had talked a lot. We talked about girls. We talked about music. We talked about dreams and our futures. We said things that made each other laugh until we cried. This was the first time we cried until we laughed. He was like a brother. He was a brother.

Tim asked if I still had those questions of where God was in my past. His faith had grown, and he was continually interested in the growth of mine. The questions lingered, though the wearing of time had dulled the jagged edges of my pain. It could be touched now, handled and held and shared, no longer cutting anyone who came in contact with it. If I had the eyes to see it then, I would have noticed the scars on Tim's own hands as he helped to carry my pain over the years.

It was good to be back at camp, and when the kids left I stayed to walk the woods alone. Years prior, this is where I had discovered God. I said a prayer and was fully redeemed. But not fully healed. Since then I've come to understand redemption and healing as an ongoing process. Only those parts of us offered can be redeemed, and only those parts of us redeemed can be healed.

Much has changed since my first time at camp. I had the same pain but not so close to the surface. Over time pain goes deeper. It becomes an empty room in our hearts and our lives are forever shaped by how we fill it. It is here where God is to be discovered, layer by layer, through the unpeeling of our pain, continually offering fresh wounds for him to enter through and heal from the inside.

The camp is situated along the cove of a small lake. The lake is filled by a stream once used to export redwoods logged from the surrounding area. Not long ago this area was an isolated community of loggers, and buildings once used as brothels were now places to encounter God. The stream entering the lake is named Ten Mile Creek, and there was a trail beginning near the cove, following the stream deep into the forest. I went for a long walk and prayed to a God I struggled to believe in. I asked him to fill the empty vessel of my heart, to expand it into something noble.

I hiked alone, putting one foot in front of the other until the beginning was a distant past. Along the trail dropped breadcrumbs of my history. The pain. The hurt. The disappointments and crushed hope. Every millstone I held onto. One by one they were swept into the stream and carried away by the current, out of the mountains and out of my life.

I entered the mystery, and in it found I was no longer alone. I stopped along a pool to try and grasp what was happening. The stream entered the pool over a small cascade and just below was a boulder slightly submerged below the surface. Behind the boulder was a rainbow trout rising for food in the current. I sat for hours wondering about this journey and why it led me here. I wondered if this peace was real and how long it would last.

Finally, I wondered what fly it would take to catch that trout.

CHAPTER 13

launch ramps

MOCHAS ARE A GATEWAY COFFEE, THE POT BROWNIES OF the coffee world. Though addicted now, I used to hate coffee almost as much as my friend Greg hates zucchini. As a teenager he declared war on the plant, sneaking into his mother's vegetable garden to cut her zucchinis at their stalks. As a form of psychological warfare, he left them to wither in place so his mom would think she couldn't grow them. He has since matured and apologized and learned to play the ukulele and he would even eat zucchini if it is ground up with chocolate.

I learned these things about him while exploring the Sierra Nevada. We were searching for a place to fish in the backcountry, so I laid out maps and cross-referenced childhood memories to circle areas from my father's fishing stories. If there was a secret fishing hole, I was determined to find it. My hope rose and fell with every bend and every pass, and though we didn't find it, I discovered new meaning in the search.

Back home Tim and I consumed copious amounts of mochas, blood running thick with caffeine and chocolate. We were trying to launch our new company and found with this new habit an ability to work late into the night, sleep a few hours, then wake up and do it again. He called the mid-afternoon practice taking a Mocha nap.

We moved into a house together with some other friends and worked from home and in cafes. We were searching for something. Purpose. Success. Completeness. It was imbedded in the dream to start a business, and like the fishing hole, I imagined that if we found it I might also find that missing piece of me locked in its secret.

Tim designed a series of T-shirts and we showed them to surf shops. The shops wanted to make orders, but we didn't have enough money to manufacture them. Our dream was stuck before it started. A friend told us about angel investing: when someone who believes in an idea makes a financial investment to help get a new company off the ground. We started looking for an angel.

During this time Tim met a girl. The fact that he met a girl was nothing new. Ever since I've known him he had a girlfriend. But for some reason things felt different with this new girl. It was how he talked about her. He said every time he saw her he wanted to pick her up and twirl her around. It sounded like a Bartles & Jaymes wine-cooler commercial.

He showed me a picture of her. She was pretty, petite, and had blonde hair, and I could see how picking her up wouldn't be a problem for him. She wasn't from Ventura, which was one of the things that attracted him to her. She didn't have the history and baggage of our small town. She gave him fresh perspective. He wanted to introduce me to her, and it made me a little nervous. I didn't want to like her. I didn't like the idea of sharing. However, within minutes of meeting Miki I liked her and knew the world had just changed.

Tim hadn't talked about his dad in a while, so I assumed things were continuing to decline in their relationship. As with any addiction, alcoholism leads to a continual series of rock bottoms, cascading like a never-ending waterfall until there is nothing left but darkness and the sensation of drowning. Yet in darkness grace still comes. For Tim's dad it came in confronting the unconditional love of a disappointed son. Tim never lost sight of who his father was, or who he was capable of being. After that day on the stairs, his dad went to an AA meeting. Then he went again and again and again and is still going today.

After Tim's dad was sober for some time, Tim invited him to visit the youth ministry. His dad hesitated before entering, then walked through the door into an uncomfortable silence. All of a sudden there was movement. One by one, the kids in the youth group stood and gave Tim's dad a standing ovation. There stood a grown man, entering this world like a newborn baby—naked and crying—in front of a group of kids who prayed for his recovery and now showered him in thunderous applause for the miracle of unyielding grace. Tim could barely watch through the tears.

In sobriety Tim's dad gained renewed interest in what his children were doing. He came across the designs Tim created for the clothing company and saw promise. He even liked Tim's idea of creating a second line called Nails, that would cater more to skateboarders. We showed him our business plan and had several follow-up discussions about how we would manufacture and where we would sell. Tim's dad decided to invest in our idea, giving us the opportunity to launch our first company. After years of wrestling with his inner demons, Tim's dad became our angel.

With the investment into South Jetty & Nails, we were able to manufacture a line of shorts and shirts and decided to build a retail kiosk to sell our clothing in the harbor on the weekends. The kiosk needed to be portable, so we designed a sort of armoire on wheels with a collapsible canopy providing shade for the merchandise and a place for us to sit and take orders. We began working on the cart in Tim's dad's muffler shop. As a kid, Tim's dad taught him to weld, and he was able to quickly weld a structural frame to which we added layers of wood and fabric and paint until the kiosk was complete.

I worked out a deal with the harbor to set up our cart along the busiest boardwalk. We both worked full-time during the week, so we prepped the clothes in the evenings and got all of our marketing materials ready to start selling once summer arrived.

When Tim called I expected it was about our new business but could tell by his tone it was something more important.

"Rog, there's a girl I want you to meet."

"Serious?"

"Yeah, dude. She's great. I think she's the one for you."

He introduced me to girls before but never with this level of confidence. He met Melissa at the college group at church and suggested we all go out so I could meet her. He said there were several things about her that were perfect for me, but didn't tell me what they were. I'd discover them soon enough. He didn't trust me enough to do this alone, so he coordinated a group of people to go out one night and made sure Melissa and I sat next to each other. We followed up after.

"What'd you think?"

"She's hot."

"I know."

"No, dude. Like, super hot."

"That's what I'm trying to tell you."

"What's wrong with her?"

"What are you talking about? Nothing."

"Why is she still available?"

"She's doing this year of no dating thing. The year's almost up."

I knew from that first moment I wanted to see more of her, but given my dating record I wasn't confident about the prospects. Tim continued to assure me and continued in his confidence that we were perfect for each other. Between Miki and Melissa, the cart and our clothing, time went quickly and soon it was summer. We were ready to launch the kiosk. Ready to launch our dreams. Ready to launch our first business.

June light fades in gradually on the harbor, filtered through a marine layer as thick and gray as fishermen's beards. In the half-light of early morning, harbor docks are busy with men checking engines and booms and winches and boys checking nets hoping to prove themselves men by day's end. In the harbor village, restaurants open early with generous servings of eggs and bacon and coffee black as boat-engine oil. They cater to an assortment of seamen—fishermen, surfers, sailors—those looking to the ocean with longing or need and those looking for a sign of hope.

By the time the marine layer burns off, the harbor will have filled with tourists and shoppers and locals bringing kids to the arcade or Coastal Cone, and there will be a line of people waiting for fish and chips at Andreas with fish fresh from commercial boats docked in front of the patio. But in the early hours, the harbor belongs to those who belong to the sea.

On good days Melissa came to visit. When she did, Tim covered for me so we could walk to the beach or get an ice cream cone. We were checking each other out while trying not to alert the other we may like them. Pre-dating is about leverage and bluffing and trying to get the first person to show their cards. Whoever plays the first hand is at a disadvantage, so we pretended as long as possible not to like each other.

Melissa was working at the church and wanted to host a summer concert. Since I lived with members of the band she wanted to book, I volunteered to talk with them and asked for her number. I already knew they couldn't do it and had no intention of actually talking to them. I just wanted her number. Tim said it was a risky maneuver but could work. She didn't seem disappointed when I broke the news that the band didn't want to play, and hoped it was a sign.

Tim helped me to come up with different reasons to get Melissa to come to the cart. "I have some ideas for your concert." "Tim's gone and I need some help covering a shift." "So-and-so is coming down and we're going to hang out. You should come too." Every time I gave her a reason she came, and every time she came was like she'd been away for a long journey and I was seeing her for the first time. It's hard to remember what she looked like. Her features blur into a feeling of how she made me seem taller. Tall enough to reach the sun and reverse the earth's axis so any day I was with her would never come to an end.

Whenever she arrived, there could be thousands of people walking in the harbor and I could instantly spot her in the crowd. I'd catch a glimpse of her hair, honey-brown and softened by the sun, light curls perfectly catching the breeze, and I'd know she'd be next to me in less than a minute. It seemed too long to wait. I'd watch as she walked, legs and hips and hair in sync, each step in time with my heartbeat. The world around her seemed still as I counted down her arrival.

Finally she was here, more beautiful than I remembered. She'd sit with me at the cart and we'd go for our walks and we'd go for our ice cream, and by the end of summer I was convinced we were ready for our first date. It was a big move, so Tim and I talked it over.

"Where are you going to take her?"

"I'm not sure. I'll think of someplace very special."

———

That summer proved several things. It proved Tim was a good matchmaker. It proved our friendship was a great foundation for a business partnership, and together there was no limit to what we could dream and do. As summer closed, our clothing company took off and we ditched the cart for a permanent surf shop in the harbor. We sub-leased a small retail section of our favorite fish burrito place and filled it with clothing.

In addition to the retail space, we sold South Jetty Boardwear in other surf shops throughout California and to build the Nails brand we began sponsoring surf and skate events. When a friend called about a concert and skateboarding demo he was promoting, we jumped at the opportunity to build the ramps. The event was a wild success.

We hung out with Jeff for the first time at a backyard party. He was a committed husband and father, a successful businessman, and volunteered with the youth ministry at church. We didn't know a lot about him, but upon meeting we liked him right away. Jeff heard that over a thousand kids showed up at the skate demo and was interested in what we were doing with the ramps. It was as if we caught lightning in a bottle. The three of us fired off ideas and quickly sketched out the concept for an indoor skate park. Over fish burritos at China Bay a few weeks later, we decided to form a partnership.

Tim and I were going away for a couple of days on a business trip, and while we were gone Jeff called to tell us he found a potential space. When we got home, we rushed straight to the warehouse to meet him for a tour. It was perfect. In an inspired moment, Jeff suggested that we stop and pray for what was about to begin. We met every week thereafter and prayed in the same spot. That spot became the largest vert ramp in the country, the cornerstone of our skate park.

More than the business, Jeff was interested in how we could posi-tively influence the youth of our area who would be drawn to the skate park. He was becoming a mentor to us. At one of our meetings he showed up more excited than usual. He thought of a name and wanted to know if we liked it. It was perfect. We would name this dream Skate Street.

For Tim and me, stepping into the empty warehouse was like

stepping into a blank canvas we could paint with every whim of our imaginations. We wanted to design our own perfect street scene. Offices would become storefronts. Support poles would become street lamps and trees. Walls would become murals of cities and landscapes enhancing never-seen-before ramps with names like "The Waterfall" and "Wave-Wall" and "Skate Mountain."

BEGINNING ON THE SKATE STREET VERT RAMP

We wanted this warehouse to transport people to a better place. A place they could drop their baggage at the door, and when they left to pick it up, to realize it was much lighter. With help from legendary skate park builders Mike Taylor and Johnny Oliver, Skate Street would become the most popular skate park in the country, attracting cameras, magazines, and the top skaters in the world.

Rumors emerged, attempting to explain who was behind Skate Street. I heard it was a front for a mysterious group taking over the industry. I also heard the skate park was being built with drug money, the two young owners doing deals all over town on their Motorola flip phones. The truth was better than any fiction. It was two best friends and a mentor who believed in them, expanding the boundaries of their dreams, inviting good friends along for the journey. The first load of lumber arrived like presents at Christmas. It was time to build.

We began demolition, and in the place of the existing structures we would build every skate ramp we ever dreamed, turning the warehouse into the largest indoor skate park in the country. These ramps would launch our careers and our lives into the full potential even we couldn't see at the time. We were only twenty-four years old and getting an opportunity to build our dream business in a thirty-three-thousand-square-foot building filled with tools and stacks of lumber. Better yet, we hired Scott and Erik, and the band was back together.

Looking back, it may not have been a good idea. I was leaning on the railing of the small cage of a scissor lift about ten feet from the ground. Tim was in front and we were riding doubles as fast as we could toward a very large wall with a group of friends cheering us on. There was another lift too. Earlier we set up a track and raced the two side by side like the great chariot race scene from *Ben Hur*. This one was clearly faster, so we liked it better.

Scissor lifts are common in construction sites, and we rented them so our contractors could reach the nearly thirty-foot ceilings of the empty warehouse. Scissor lifts are less commonly used for racing and even less as wrecking balls. But these walls had to come down, and Tim thought a scissor lift would be a fun way to do it, so long as it was the faster one. As we got closer to the wall, I was having doubts.

Unlike other construction tools, scissor lifts are not that fast. In

THE WAVE WALL LOOKING TOWARD THE BANK AND EMBARCADERO STEPS

VERT RAMP AND WATERFALL ROLL IN

fact, belt sanders are much faster. That's where the racing began. We had both Craftsman and Makita belt sanders and were arguing about which was faster. To settle the matter we plugged them both into hundred-foot extension cords and starting at the back of the warehouse, simultaneously jammed them in the on position, and let them grind across the empty concrete floor until reaching the finish line on the other side. The Makita was much faster, which is why we named the stray dog hanging around Makita and took her home. Tim really wanted a dog, so everything was working out perfectly.

During construction I gave Tim a strange design quest.

"I want to build roll-ins on every ramp."

"Why?"

"I'm afraid to drop in."

DROPPING IN

"What do you mean you're afraid? You're an owner of Skate Street. You can't be afraid to drop in."

"I don't know what to tell you. It freaks me out."

"Fine. I'll teach you."

He instructed me to position my skateboard so the ramp was directly under the board's tail, with the back wheels snug against the transition of the ramp and all my weight on the back foot. To drop in I needed to firmly plant my feet on the board and transition my weight forward. Most importantly, I needed to grab the nose of my board, not letting go until I was through the transition. The key was to commit and hold tightly to the thing I was committing to. Holding on increased the likelihood of surviving the drop in. If I let go mid drop, I'd find myself flat on my back, wondering how in the world I got there.

I stood frozen atop the ramp. Everything I dreamed of lay before me. Friendship. Skate Street. Love. Still, I was afraid to commit. Finally, after some coaxing from Tim, I dropped into the ramp.

But the commitment still freaked me out.

CHAPTER 14

fish tacos

I'M NOT SURE WHY ANYONE WOULD CONSIDER TAKING A super hot girl to Boston Market on their first date or why the super hot girl would say yes to such a proposal or insist on paying for her half of the naturally glazed rotisserie chicken. At best, dating is confounding as a Rubik's Cube. Get the colors to match on one side and your dating life is better than most. Get the colors to match on two sides and you're a freakin' Casanova.

Before we got in line, Melissa informed me she'd be paying for her half of the meal, and I was already confused about our relationship. I thought this was a date but maybe it wasn't.

Maybe she's going through something. Maybe she just wants my advice on other boys. Maybe I'm the nice guy who takes girls to Boston Market for a comfortable buffet and listens intently as they spill their guts about who they really like and what they need to do to get his attention and since I know him so well could I maybe talk with him. Maybe I'm that guy.

Maybe she thinks I'm gay. I've been told by other girls that I'm a good listener and I have kind eyes. I thought that's what they wanted. To be listened to. To be understood. Maybe they just want to be listened to by their gay friends. Maybe she just really likes the gravy. Which, who can blame her? It does travel down smooth.

We were staring through the sneeze guard choosing side dishes and I was trying to compensate for my good listening skills by determining if green beans or mashed potatoes would be more manly, and I found myself already annoyed by her self-reliance. I began to wonder if she was just saying she wanted to pay for her bill but was secretly hoping I would. As with all things in a dating relationship, this was probably a test. It was a way to see what kind of a man I was. Guys have been taught for years they are supposed to be gentlemen and pay for dates. It's an American tradition. If I caved now, I would be disappointing every grandfather in the country. We were nearing the end of the buffet line and my confusion turned to annoyance now turned to anger.

Who does this girl think she is? On behalf of all men who have bravely walked the buffet line before, I'm paying for this bill. The world is confusing enough.

We got to the cash register and the cashier was about to ring us up and I was begging him with my kind, listening eyes to help a brother out and I could tell we were connecting and he got the situation and I reached for my wallet.

"Will that be together or separate?"

"Together."

"Separate."

"Together."

She looked at me, then at the cashier, then back at me and at the same time the cashier and I both knew.

"Separate."

Dating is awkward. Two strangers checking each other out, trying to see their strengths and flaws and trying hard not to let the other know they are looking and speculating about whether to hang out with them for lunch or coffee or dinner and a movie, and wondering if their values are similar, and if they have a good job, and if they like their parents and Jesus and long walks on the beach, and wondering what they look like naked.

Generally speaking, the opposite sexes are looking for two completely different things in a dating relationship. We both have our lists, formed from childhood by watching our parents and expanding over time by dreams, fairy tales, and hard realities. Our lists grow into a description of a future mate only to be realized by a Greek god or goddess. The idea that somehow, in whatever amount of time the girl allows, and whatever amount of time the guy can get away with, we are able to come to some understanding of lifelong compatibility is crazy. At best we can only hope to see something honest about the other. Something true. And decide if that truth in them will complete our own, shaping us daily into something closer to what we are meant to become.

Early in our dating relationship Melissa and I talked about our parents. What usually ended in an awkward conversation about my dad became something different. Over the years this dialogue became a scripted play. I played my part of the fatherless boy wandering defenseless in a dangerous world, then on cue the listener of my sad story had some sincere words of compassion along with courteous follow-up questions. "What was he like? Do you miss him? Do you look like him?"

This would go on long enough to satisfy obligations of empathy but not long enough to draw me into anything revealing the depths of grief lurking below the surface of these questions. I told Melissa my story and was waiting for her to play her role, but it never came. There was empathy but something greater behind it. Something in her eyes. And I knew that she knew.

Instead of any follow-up questions, she told me her story. Her mom was also troubled. She also thought she had something to do with it. She also prayed for God to make her mom better. She also stayed up late, listening to every sound, looking for a clue to what the world would be like when she woke the next morning. She also didn't know what to do on Mother's Day. Her world also fell apart when Melissa was sixteen. Her mom killed herself. When she finished there was a comfortable silence. Our experiences immediately bonded us in something deeper.

We are fashioned by our grief. Formed in its fires, features chiseled by pain. In grief character is tested. In pain we are revealed. Melissa and I were being exposed to each other through wounds and scars and perhaps even more through what wasn't said. Sometimes the deepest truth is found in what's been edited from our narratives. She wasn't full of bitterness or anger or any other corruption of her pain. Her pain was making her into something better.

It struck me that the actions of our parents somehow connected us. That the ugliest and darkest moments of our lives were being knit together into something beautiful. It gave us a head start in our relationship. A perspective on what was really important. And what wasn't. As my relationship with Melissa grew, I found myself becoming thankful for a history I typically tried to ignore. This history made me more patient. More kind. Perhaps the pain was making me better too.

A widely attended skate and surf show was coming up in San Diego, so Tim and I decided to go promote the opening of the skate park. But first we'd get some surf in Mexico. Some friends told us we should check out a place called K38, located thirty-eight kilometers south of the border, which we mistakenly confused with miles. Rather than turn back we headed to another surf spot, found an empty beach to camp for the night, and listened to waves crashing darkly in the distance.

Life was becoming a whirlwind with an eager public, a growing staff, and news cameras at the skate park almost daily reporting on the exciting new business created by two twenty-four-year-olds. On top of that, Tim proposed to Miki and asked me to be the best man in his wedding. The world was changing fast, and we needed a moment for it to slow down.

Over the next couple of days, we surfed empty waves near quiet villages smelling of salt and fish. After, we'd find an open-air restaurant and spend evenings barefoot and shirtless, eating freshly caught fish tacos, washing them down with bottled Coca-Colas as the sun hung summerlike over the Pacific. Someone once told me heaven would be better than anything we could dream of on earth. He challenged me to imagine the best moment of my life, to close my eyes and hold it in my memory. This would be the starting point of eternity.

In that *palapa* with Tim it wasn't hard to imagine. Warm waters. Right point breaks. An endless horizon of waves rising through soft filters of sunset light. Heaven would feel like summer.

It came as a surprise that I would like Tim better the more time he spent with Miki, though hearing "Tim and Miki" instead of "Tim and Rog" took a little getting used to. I was becoming just Rog. Through the engagement Tim and I remained roommates, Melissa moved in with Miki, and we started spending all our free time together as couples. Melissa and I agreed to meet Tim and Miki at a favorite restaurant.

There's a certain progression to new relationships. It includes important milestones to be mutually understood with conversations carefully documenting where a couple is in any one moment along the relationship continuum. It's very precise. It's similar to the large thermometer graph at an elementary school fundraiser where the temperature is colored in red to show how close the school is to achieving the fund-raising goal. It's updated regularly, and with every new donation someone eagerly colors in more red to show the precise visual cue to where the campaign is in relationship to the goal. The only difference between the women's relationship thermometer and the school fund-raiser version is the wedding ring on top.

We had had the talk. At least part of it. Melissa invited me over to breakfast and ambushed me with a discussion about where our relationship was going. Knowing my lack of confidence, Tim had recently pulled Melissa aside and advised if she had any feelings for me she would need to tell me. Explicitly. Tim didn't trust me enough in a relationship to do the right thing and continued to meddle in my love affairs. He told her left to my own devices I wouldn't get it. I wouldn't get the clues. I wouldn't get the nuances.

So she took matters into her own hands and over pancakes proceeded to communicate how she felt about me. I was stunned. Then relieved. Though in the excitement of it all I forgot to reciprocate my feelings toward her, breaking all relationship progression etiquettes until finally a week later I realized my grave error and told her I liked her too. It was now official. We were dating and could move to the next step in our relationship: holding hands.

On their own, hands are not all that sexy. You don't hear guys in the locker room talking about the hands that girl had. *Sports Illustrated* will never do a special release of a magazine featuring pictures of women's hands on exotic Caribbean beaches. They're the working class of our bodies. In a guy's relationship-status thermometer, which is measured much differently than the previously described women's version, holding hands is not even first base. It's more like the batter on deck. But as an important visual symbol of our new relationship status, on the way to the restaurant I grabbed her hand. The world slowed, reversed its axis, and every step from that point was free from the confines of gravity.

I'd never held something so holy. I slowly wrapped my fingers around hers and knew all previous measures of pain or pleasure would forever now be qualified by the feeling of Melissa's hand in mine. As we walked I felt every ridge and valley of her palm. They fit as a key, unlocking the closet door where skeletons of hope and love had long been stuffed away. On the way to the restaurant I could feel the soft underside of her wrist touch against mine, ever so lightly, almost unknowable, like the changing of the wind. Like the doorway of eternity.

I longed for her fingers and her hands and the rest of what came after. I longed for the restaurant to disappear so we might walk forever. Past whatever plans we had for the night. Past whatever may come tomorrow. I longed for my closet of pain to spill into the night and pave the road with every memory of every disappointment so we could dance upon it.

The skate park was nearing completion, but there was still one ramp Tim and I wanted to build together. In a corner of the warehouse we reserved a space for a mini ramp. We discussed plans and decided it would be four feet high with a mellow transition—the slope from the top of the ramp to the bottom would be gentle so beginners could ride it easier. We framed

DECK — COPING

TRANSITION

FLAT BOTTOM

SECTION OF MINI RAMP

the transitions and flat bottom and were moving on to build the decks. Tim worked on one side and I worked on the other. I laid out the frame and grabbed a hammer and some nails. I tapped in the nail a little bit to get it started and paused to aim the hammer.

It made me think of building our first ramp on top of Kmart Hill, under the shade of the trees, looking over dirt tracks and jumps covering what was once a dump and what eventually became an upscale neighborhood and shopping center. Someone saw potential in a piece of land others passed over and one day broke ground, put hammer to a nail, and the Kmart hills were transformed.

My life once felt passed over. Then one day I met Tim. He saw potential, and on top of that holy hill gave me a hammer and nail to build that potential together. In this corner of what would become a world-renowned skate park launching us into success we'd never dreamed of, I aimed the hammer and with a swift and confident swing drove in the nail. And another. And another. And with a symphony of power tools in the background, we finished the mini ramp, so closely resembling our beginning.

Skate Street was ready to open.

Tim arranged with a company sponsoring the skate park for each guy in his wedding to have a new pair of shoes. We'd also be wearing tuxedo tops with shorts, which was great since it was an unusually warm day. When it came time for dancing at the reception, I watched from the table with the others in the wedding party as Tim danced with his new bride. He was as happy as I'd ever seen him.

I fumbled nervously through the toast and my official best man duties came to a close. I was talking to the Skate Street crew about what would happen while Tim was on his honeymoon when I saw a circle form on the dance floor. There was some wild cheering. The DJ was playing some old-school music from our junior high years, and I wedged myself in the circle to see what was happening. As I got closer I could see arms twirling on the dance floor. At the end of each arm were some poofy white shirtsleeves.

Tim was doing the windmill.

CHAPTER 15

safe harbor

THERE'S A FAMILIAR FEELING YOU GET WHEN THINGS ARE going right in a relationship. It's as recognizable as the thing you know you ought to do when you have a choice to do it or not. Shortly into our relationship I had that feeling. Wherever Melissa was, on the other side of the world or sitting next to me, it was never close enough. There was a place she wanted to take me, someplace special to her.

Melissa's stepdad still lived at the ranch that belonged to her mother while she was alive, and on the ranch was an arena where horses ran. Bordered by oaks and shrubs, it sat in a shallow valley where warm breezes carried soft scents of sagebrush growing wildly on the hillsides. In the middle of the arena was a fire and blankets and a place to watch the stars. We talked late into the night wondering where our stories fit into the constellations. Under the eternal gazes of Virgo and Orion, I leaned over to kiss her and was ushered into the heavens.

Just as Tim predicted, she was the one. Still, I was afraid to drop in.

I read somewhere that along the upper coast of Maine there was a place where the sun first touched the US, and thought the first light of the country might clear the fog of marriage. Entrenched in my doubts was a fear that if I truly loved Melissa she would be taken away. One of the side effects of losing someone early in life is a fear that everything I truly loved would be lost. As a way to guard against the potential loss of some great joy, I keep a safe distance from it. I flirt with it but don't commit. I am afraid of joy. Now, for the first time, I feared the loss more.

Tim and I discussed the issue over coffee.

"What's your plan?"

Saying it out loud made it sound a little crazier than it did in my head.

"I'm going to land in Boston, get a car and drive north."

He knew me well enough to know I needed this trip to sort things out. I'd been thinking about the trip for weeks but didn't plan very well. I began to realize it shortly after landing in Boston.

"What do you mean you have no cash?"

The lady in the tollbooth wasn't getting it. I explained the whole situation again while honking vehicles piled up behind my rental car. I told her I just flew in from California where there was a girl and she could be the one but I wasn't sure and I was on this trip to watch the sunrise over the ocean hoping it would help me figure out if I should marry her.

"Don't you have oceans in California?"

"Look, I don't know what to tell you. I don't have any cash."

"You can mail it. Here's an envelope."

I drove north through New England fishing villages with October blue reflecting brightly off the Atlantic, a stunning backdrop to the crimson and yellow leaves of sugar maples along the shore. I stayed as close to the ocean as possible. It was my only bearing.

Shortly after crossing into Maine I spotted a peninsula and drove to the end of the cape, where I discovered a lighthouse known as the Cape Neddick Light and camped for the night. The lighthouse has been in continual service since 1879, and watching it signal to passersby at sea I couldn't help but think of all the ships passing in the night, thankful for the safety of the light. I thought of the noble purpose of lighthouses, to warn sailors of danger and point them toward safe harbor.

I thought of the dangers of my life. About my tendencies toward isolation and the craggy cliffs along the shore of the island I might become. I thought about these things as I sat along the rocks across the short channel to the light. It faced bravely toward the vast ocean, staring over an endless sea in the confidence of its purpose.

I wanted certainty about the situation. How can you make a decision as big as marriage without a little more certainty about life? Marriage isn't a drive-through latte on the way to Maine where you know if it doesn't taste right you can pour it out the window. Marriage isn't like coffee shops. You don't hop in one that looks promising and try out the menu, then discard a half-finished drink because the espresso was too weak or too strong or you were still full from breakfast.

Though it may seem like it, marriage isn't born from American consumerism. It's born from an older time and carries with it a challenge to all men: "Can you truly love? Are you capable of such feats?" Marriage is a weapon, sharp as any sword, cutting both the world and the man who uses it, wounding and shaping him into something better. It's a test of our mettle, to see how well we can love and give and be fulfilled through the loving. I wasn't sure if I was such a man or if I could achieve such greatness.

I stayed the night at the lighthouse, sleeping on the shore. Though I didn't sleep much, I found my answer. It was carried in the rays of light, answering the distressed call of an empty heart lost at sea. The next morning I called Tim.

"How's your road trip?"

"Great."

"And?"

"I'm going to ask Melissa to marry me."

"That's the best decision you've ever made."

"I need you to be my best man."

"That's your second best decision."

For an engagement present Tim framed a picture of me surfing on his bachelor-party trip. Our mentor Jeff made a connection for us to go to the Channel Islands on a private boat with a captain who knew where to find the best surf, and with a cook named Fish. On clear days the islands are visible off our coastline. They are about thirteen miles and a world away. Making our way across the deep water of the channel, the captain let us take turns driving the boat, and I was in the cockpit with Tim talking about what marriage would be like and what life would be like after and what the surf would be like once we got to the island.

There is a point on the way to the islands where a fog often lingers, and you can no longer navigate by land. When we got there, the captain gave us the bearings of where we were headed and showed us how to stay true to the compass. When we don't know what's ahead, it's often the compass readings from someone who has been there that give us confidence to make the journey.

I asked Tim how he knew for sure that marriage was the right decision, but as I was asking him I realized I was really asking for myself. How can you trust love? Love comes like these dolphins swimming below the bow of the boat. Jumping and playing, putting on a spectacular display, then disappearing only to leave you standing on the edge peering into the deep, eyes stinging from salted spray. Love comes. Love goes. I could believe it existed, but I couldn't believe it would stay. Tim reassured me it would. He just knew.

All that lay before us was sky and sea and hope of waves and love and an overwhelming feeling of thankfulness. The water reflected the color of the sky, and the sky lifted the blue from the water's surface.

We were floating between two mirrors, and if you looked far enough there was no separation of heaven and earth. Water seeks its own level, and we seek the water to find ours. I knew Tim was right about love because it had already been demonstrated in the years of our friendship. I could find comfort in that. The boat continued to carry us toward an unknown future forever fading into a blue horizon.

The picture he gave me as an engagement present was a reminder of that moment. Attached to the picture was a handwritten letter. Perhaps more than anyone, Tim knew my deepest fears and regrets, and one by one he addressed them in this letter. He wrote with an authority to set me free. They were the words I'd wanted to hear from my father. They were the words I needed.

At the end of the letter he made a confession that gave me a confidence I'd yet to have. He told me of talent I possessed that he'd admired, even envied. All these years I'd considered myself lucky to be in his shadow. For the same number of years, he felt lucky to be in mine. He went on to say how proud he was of me and what a gift God had given me in Melissa. I was in tears by the end of the letter. These were the good words of an even better man.

Weddings are expensive. I hadn't thought much about them, and whenever I did I assumed it was just put on a suit, have a bunch of people show up, and throw a little party after. Apparently I'm wrong. Super wrong. The first thing I was wrong about was thinking the wedding was just one day. It's a whole season. Like football season. Dating is only preseason. Guys like preseason because it's all fun and games and the coach hasn't really engaged. They get lulled into thinking the stakes aren't that high and mistakenly assume when they propose things will go on the way they did.

The official ending of preseason is when you have the last of the dating talks resulting in either a very expensive ring or a parachute. Guys think this is the end. It's just the beginning. The proposal is only the kickoff on opening day. The wedding ceremony is the Super Bowl, and if a guy wants to be invited to the party after, he needs to learn the game.

I looked to Tim for some advice, but he basically said I was on my own. Any man who has survived a wedding is hesitant to go back in. It's the one territory where even the toughest Marine will leave a man behind. He told me my only job was to make sure the bride is happy. A wedding is its own solar system orbiting the bride. She is the sun, and the trick to surviving is to keep her shining just the right amount. Too much heat and planets will be scorched. Too little and earth freezes over and we all starve to death. It's a delicate business.

This is a time where guys shouldn't be thinking about costs. But nobody told me that. I wasn't quite prepared for the cost of it all, and since we were paying for a lot of it ourselves, I was looking for ways to help ease the pain. After brainstorming several ideas, I finally came up with something I thought would work. In fact, it was brilliant. It was the kind of idea that could change the wedding industrial complex forever. I asked Tim to coffee to go over the idea with him. He was hesitant to show up.

"I've got a great idea on how we can pay for our wedding."

I could tell he was skeptical but he agreed to hear me out.

"I could sell ads in our wedding brochure."

"You mean program?"

"Sure. You could design it, right?"

"Have you run this idea by Melissa?"

"Think I should? I thought of surprising her with it."

By his look I could tell he didn't think it was the best idea and there was no way he would be accomplice to anything involving a wedding *brochure.*

"Fine, I'll run it by her. She'll think it's a great idea."

That was the last idea I contributed to the wedding.

When the wedding day arrived, we vowed to each other a loyalty separated only by death and a love to last even longer. Love, the greatest of emotions, humbles itself to meet us at the first breaths of our awkward beginnings. It gives of itself. Purely it gives. Without hesitation. Without regret. We age and age and take and take, and yet it gives more. True love is ever expanding. It delights in the giving, and gives in such abundance that its full measure can never be received. And so love returns to itself greater than it started.

When we truly love we experience the eternalness of God. This love is forever. It's the only thing that lasts. On the first night of the rest of our lives, I carried Melissa through the doorway of a discount hotel room and laid her onto a bed where I fell heavy into her arms and became immortal.

We settled into time, our new home and our new routines. In the morning Melissa set me sail as I left for work, slapping my butt on the way out of the house, providing extra momentum for whatever headwinds I would face that day. A man held in the strength of a wife's love can do far more than he ever dreamed. While I was out to sea I fished and fought and cast about and longed for home. When the time came to set the compass to my true north, I told her I was coming, and knew she'd be watching.

I turned from the main channel onto the side road where I saw our white-shingled house glowing in the reflected light of an afternoon sun. Branches of our Jacaranda tree caught a coastal breeze, sending bright purple flowers singing and dancing in slow, soft descent, quietly landing in the lush shade of a fresh-cut lawn. I began up our winding brick walkway perfumed by the snow-white flowers of bordering jasmine, the bouquet that helped sell the house. The world had gone gold and green, purple and white.

Our home smelled of love and our love smelled of spring. Before I was to the door her arms reached for me. Beyond the threshold. Beyond the shelter of the porch. Her arms extended like breakwaters into the ocean. They calmed the waters and drew me in. I set my anchor into her heart.

For she was my safe harbor.

CHAPTER 16

Nashvegas

WHEN YOU FIRST GET MARRIED YOU FEEL AS IF YOU'RE IN
a movie. You've seen the previews and know the key moments; you
just don't know when they arrive. Our new life in our new house was
everything the previews promised. We even built a garden, and in it
began growing tomatoes and eggplant and bell peppers, and around it
grew the charming life of newlyweds.

One day after work I entered our newly married movie set to find
Melissa in the living room waiting for me with a card. In it was the
news that she was pregnant. She had sweetly arranged the card with
candles and flowers on the mantel. I of course didn't notice the candles
and opened the card hoping it might be a gift certificate to Home
Depot. It wasn't. We had a conversation about it.

"Really?"

"Yes."

"Are you sure?"

"Yes."

"But are you really sure?"

"Yes. I took several tests and they were all positive."

Long pause.

"That's. Umm. Awesome?"

By tests she meant one of those sticks telling a woman if she's pregnant. I'd heard rumors of those sticks but have always been a little dubious. At first I thought they were used like an oil dipstick, getting dipped up to the baby areas and coming out with a mark on the hash tags, indicating whether a woman was pregnant or if more oil was needed. It didn't seem scientific enough to be accurate, and a proper response to this kind of news required certainty. I didn't realize at the time that the actual scientific method for determining the single most life-altering event in the history of our marriage would be for my beautiful new wife to pee on a stick. I felt much better. She was confident and had several sticks to prove it. She gave me a hug. I wondered if she had washed her hands.

It wasn't a total surprise. We had talked about kids while dating and I always thought I'd be excited, but now things got real and my excite-o-meter was leaning a little more toward terrified. How could I be a dad? Sure, I understood the science between sex and pregnancy. But sex doesn't prepare one for fatherhood. In fact, it's the furthest thing from your mind during sex. It is really, really, really far. It's not even on your mind afterward.

Afterward you think about food. Usually Pringles, but sometimes a sandwich. And while you get up and make a sandwich, the thought that one of your little sperms is at this very moment swimming upstream like salmon in search of fertile spawning grounds isn't even close to your mind. In fact, the only thing on your mind is wondering where the heck your wife hid the mayonnaise.

Oh, it's next to the mustard.

Any excitement of pregnancy was held hostage by questions regarding my ability to father. I supposed if it was a boy I could teach him how to shave and ride a skateboard and a surfboard and a snowboard and tie a good fishing knot. After that it was all a little blurry. *I'm not qualified. I'm not ready. I didn't have a dad.* And finally, there it is. The real issue. I was a fatherless child wondering how to father a child.

I still missed my dad. His loss was a weed in our perfectly tended tomato garden. When it came up I pulled it and it was gone for a while, leaving things looking perfect again. But then it spread underground, coming up by the eggplant. In each season of life the weed grew from a different place of my heart, and though I pulled the top I couldn't get to the root because doing so would require my heart's removal. Instead I identified and labeled it as it broke the surface. I knew what the issue was. I had no reference point for being a dad.

Fortunately I was able to distract myself by the success of the skate park. We were getting regular coverage in skateboarding magazines, and Skate Street was considered by our industry to be one of the best skate parks in the world. I got a call from a video game company asking if they could model our skate park in a sequel to a popular skateboarding game, and they came to motion capture Tony Hawk doing a checklist of signature tricks on our vert ramp. Skate Street would be a level in the video game *Tony Hawk Pro Skater 2*. With this came more news coverage and more notoriety.

Soon Tim and I were getting phone calls to meet with investors and developers who wanted to have skate parks in their malls and shopping centers and warehouses, and we traveled the country to visit these places and meet with these people, and it seemed there'd be no end to our success.

Success is an imitation substance, like drinking soda instead of water when you're thirsty. You can drink large amounts, but at the end, your body will not be satisfied. Still, I wanted more and more of it, even if the appearance was greater than the content. I began measuring success by what I read about Skate Street in newspapers and magazines and started down the slippery slope of defining myself by my work.

In truth, I had no more to do with Skate Street's success than a wildflower has to do with a bloom after a spring rain. I had been planted in a place, and whether you've come to believe the place we are planted has to do with luck or a divine force or the skill of our making is beside the point. No matter how I was planted, I had no control of the rain.

———————

We were going through a pen phase. On special occasions Tim and I would give each other cool pens we found while shopping our favorite office supply stores. It peaked when he gave me a special Montblanc pen for my birthday. It could have been a fake, but I used it with all the pomp of an original. I also had a thing for attaché bags, but Tim didn't share my enthusiasm. I used my special pens to draft a plan to build Skate Streets throughout the country. I even made a deal with God that if he wanted to partner with me, I'd cut him in on the ministry action. All he had to do was get the right people to call. I'd take it from there.

To prepare I read every book prescribing seven steps or forty days to achieve success and purpose. I followed the advice of the books and strategized how to grow the business and become the successful person I was destined to be. If I couldn't find the secret fishing hole, I'd create my own. The plan would take years to achieve, but I figured by the time I was forty I would have it all. Financial success. Spiritual enlightenment. Six-pack abs.

Tim and I divided responsibilities. I handled calls from outside interests while he managed the day-to-day of the skate park. One of the calls I received was from a group in Nashville called Rocketown. They were launching a large youth entertainment and outreach facility and heard of Skate Street from a recent CNN story about a nontraditional "Skate Church" we hosted with a youth pastor friend. They offered for me to visit Nashville to see what they were up to. The group had a big vision of how to influence the lives of kids, and though I felt a faint voice telling me to go, I couldn't see how it would advance the rest of my goals. I turned them down. I reminded God of our deal and began to wonder if he was really up for the task.

The biggest names in pro skating dropped by Skate Street on a regular basis to do photo shoot sessions, train for the X Games, or compete in our Plywood Paradise competitions. Just as impressive, local skaters innovated new ways to skate a skate park. They were led by Nick pulling rodeo flips off the stage kicker, Josh executing street-styled technical tricks on the mini ramp, and Gavin, masked to hide his identity, flying through the park like a superhero.

Like most locals, Mark began skating the first day we opened and continued to skate every day after. He quickly became the corner-stone of Skate Street's local scene. He was inspirational not only for his skating but also his positive personality in light of the difficulties he'd already persevered through at a young age. Every time Mark came through the door Skate Street became better for it. The staff was in shock when we got the phone call. Mark was involved in a horrible accident. His girlfriend died in his arms. Skate Street was the first place he thought to call, and to help him recover we gave him a job. With Mark the staff began to feel like family.

Sometimes family hurts us the worst. We noticed the register coming up short at closing. It was hard to believe one of our staff members, one of our family, could be stealing from us. We didn't want to believe it, and while watching security tapes I could tell Tim was thinking, *Please, don't be Derrick.*

Derrick was in his midtwenties and had worked with us for months. He'd struggled in the past and was trying to get his life back on track. Tim spent a lot of time with Derrick and was proud of his progress. He had a contagious smile and was well loved by customers and staff alike. The room went silent as we watched Derrick pull money out of the register and slide it in his pocket. I looked over to Tim, and his head was in his hands. A moment later he broke the silence.

"I'll do it."

The next day Derrick was gone, and I never saw him at the skate park again. I didn't see Tim the next day either.

The time came to hear our baby's heartbeat. My surprise turned to excitement, and I wanted to be on top of things. Melissa put me in charge of the baby's room, and we decided to find out the sex so I'd know whether to decorate it with pink or blue surfboards. We also started a list of names, and I had visions of a little Savannah or Hunter bundled in my arms, cooing and smiling with newborn hair smelling perfect as earth's first day. The nurse helped Melissa get comfortable, and the doctor came in to administer the ultrasound.

There was no heartbeat. Silence sterilized our joy. The doctor gave some instructions and sent us home.

The house was quiet. Our instructions were to wait; Mother Nature would take over from here. I walked from room to room looking for a distraction, checking on Melissa, then making another lap. I made tea. I organized baby supplies. I waited.

There is no comfort to fill an empty space where once there was life. I tried to be as sad as my wife and tried to cry and tried to hide the secret feelings of relief. In the shadow of our secrets grows our shame. I lacked courage to become the one thing I desperately searched for my whole life. A father. It was a confrontation with the limitations of my character, and I lost. And the shame grew.

Over time, once comfortable routines fit like someone else's clothing, and though Skate Street continued to succeed, the excitement settled into the daily care of Tim's management. Everything that used to take two of us now only took one. Life felt redundant. I continued to take calls from outside interests and found myself once again talking to a board member from the Nashville group. I was ready for a change. I tried to envision any scenario of including Tim, but even if there were a possibility, Tim wouldn't be leaving. He felt called to Ventura. If I went it would be my first adventure without him.

Tim and I developed a Friday afternoon ritual where when the mood struck, which was predictable and usually around 3:30, someone would ask, "What time is it?" and after the immediate response "Beer-thirty!" we'd be off to the pier. For much of our town's history, we've bragged about having the longest wooden pier in California. The problem of boasting "mine is longer than yours" is you forever have to defend your position. Every few years we'd get a winter storm producing waves powerful enough to swallow the pier, and they reclaimed enough wood to remove those bragging rights.

Eventually the city reinforced the pier with steel and at the base of the pier built a restaurant. On the second floor of that restaurant was a bar high above the water, where from the outer corner of the balcony you could look back onto the city curving bananalike around the base of the hills, or look down the pier pointing into the Pacific and order a beer that sometimes came with a small loaf of bread. There you could talk about the things you didn't want to talk about but knew you'd feel better about in the telling.

We sat at our favorite table and from our seats could see the beach where we got into our first fight. Beyond, breakwaters sheltered boats as they entered the harbor where our first business launched. In the other direction I could see the grassy lawn of the point with Pipes and Hobos in the distance and in front the mellow waves of the Cove, breaking all the way into the staircase leading to where Charlie's used to be. I hesitated a moment, then told Tim.

"I'm going to take that job in Nashville."

Life is just an observation until action is taken. Then it becomes yours.

"It's a good opportunity. I think you should take it."

Tim listed the reasons this was a good move for me, and they sounded better coming from him. We talked about my fears of leaving. He told me he'd always be there. We talked about my doubts of pulling off this new job. He told me I was good enough. We raised our glasses. Portraits of our history hung in the background.

I landed in Oz where everything changed. The land. The weather. My dreams, fluttering like fireflies after a summer rain.

"Welcome to Nashvegas!"

Ben's handshake was full of all the generosity of the South. Growing up on the beach of Southern California, when someone talked about the south I assumed they were referring to Mexico. It made me think of tacos. I love tacos. I told that to Ben. He took me to the San Antonio Taco Company, and like many conversations to come, began with, "Now, these won't be like California, but . . ."

The tacos in Nashville are different. They are also great. So are the people. I developed a taste and realized it's all in the seasoning. Equal parts grace and hospitality. It took about a week and a half to develop lifelong friends. Life so far had been a familiar road. I knew what I wanted and where I was going. This was a left turn. A detour. I found quickly that in the South, detours and back roads were often a shortcut to what's really important. We spent a lot of time on porches where Ben taught me the art of catching fireflies.

Melissa liked it too. For the first time in our marriage it was just the two of us. We lived in Franklin, a small, historic town south of Nashville. Franklin established itself as a city before California became a state, and Main Street is lined with buildings predating the Civil War and trees with leaves signaling the changes of each season. There are a lot of parades.

At the coffee shop on the corner of town we would sit and watch young families push strollers and old couples hold hands as they window-shopped, and when snow fell lightly and gathered on the stone wall of the church across the street, it felt like we lived in a snow globe. Surrounding the town were the rolling hills of middle Tennessee, dotted with horse farms and lined with long wooden fences hewn from the hardwoods growing along the perimeters. When I wasn't working, we loved to drive these back roads and end up in even smaller towns to buy chocolate malts. None of the roads were straight. They meandered with the land, giving a sense of connection with it. The whole region is rooted.

Rocketown is a vision of Michael W. Smith, a music celebrity living just south of Nashville. He would see kids hanging out on the street with nowhere to go and wanted to provide a place for them. The same time we were running Skate Street in Ventura, they were running a small music venue outside of Nashville. Michael wanted to combine both those elements, and more. He envisioned a place where kids would not only want to hang out on a Friday or Saturday night, but also where they would come after school to work with mentors in dance or music or math. It would be a place to meet the unmet needs of youth. It was a big vision.

My role would begin with developing the skate park portion of the forty-thousand-square-foot downtown warehouse, and it quickly grew into helping with the entire vision and running it once it opened. It was a high-profile vision, including other music celebrities and international CEOs, and with President George Bush Senior acting as the chairman of the capital campaign. I was clearly in over my head, and without Tim I felt unqualified and alone. I missed him.

After Rocketown opened I called Tim, and he was as excited for me as he would have been if he were opening it. I gave him every detail about the skate park and music venue and sent him photos. In exchange he filled me in about the church he was helping start. He had recently connected with Greg, a local youth pastor who married a high school friend of ours, and together they were dreaming of a community who would follow God differently. Wholly. It was a community of people known as the Bridge. As he spoke of it, there was a sense of calling in his voice. Also a rootedness. The roots he planted in Ventura interwove with this community of people that he talked of. That he loved.

Years earlier I was driving alone through the mountains of Utah and came across a stand of aspen trees in the early fall. For hours I hiked under a canopy of leaves that were reaching to grab yellow directly from the sun and softly radiate it to me below. The trail seemed to never end, and I later learned that this stand of aspens was one of the largest living organisms on earth. The roots of the trees grew toward each other and entwined into a single living body. They became interdependent for nutrients. For life. As Tim described what was happening back home, it reminded me of this.

Still searching for success and purpose, I tried fitting Rocketown into my plan and became frustrated when I couldn't. My plan was slipping. In a final act of desperation one night after closing, I was alone in the music venue and inquired of God why he brought me to Nashville. I'm not used to getting direct answers back. I'm usually thinking it will come later in a voice mail. Probably as a blocked call so God isn't annoyed by me calling back every ten minutes and hanging up until I finally get through.

But this time I received an immediate strong impression and had a feeling it was God. So after a brief catch-up on how things were going and about the weather, we talked a bit. I've never heard the voice of God but a question impressed into my heart.

"Remind me of your plan again?"

"The plan is that I build Skate Street. I mean, we build Skate Street. Then I/we build another and another so kids all over the country will be able to go to one and everybody will know how awesome I am/we are."

I looked around, and for the first time things became clear. I was standing in the middle of the plan I/we came up with. A former run-down warehouse on the dirty side of town, still bearing scars of its former life, transformed into a space dedicated to transforming the lives of those encountering it. It was exactly what Jeff, Tim, and I prayed about every week in the spot that became our first vert ramp. It was exactly what Tim and I talked about at the end of a week of sold-out sessions. It was exactly what I asked God to use me to do. Only it wasn't called Skate Street and I wasn't in control. And it wasn't about me.

But God was working through me, and he was at work in the lives of those coming through the doors. And at the exact same time he was doing the exact same thing in Ventura. I was running this one. Tim was running the other. Though I didn't recognize it, the plan was perfect. This detour wasn't a detour at all. It was a test of my character, to see if I had the courage to follow a faint voice saying, "Turn here." The desires given Tim and I would be fulfilled, even if it wasn't in the package I was expecting. It wouldn't be the last time.

I told this all to Tim in one of our routine phone calls. At the end he asked if anything else was going on. Life's events seemed real once I shared them with Tim, so I was hesitant to say. I wasn't sure if I wanted to face the prospects of another disappointment, so not saying anything would be easier. I wouldn't have to get my hopes up or once again deal with the disappointment. Good friends know better. And they're not afraid to ask. Again he pushed.

"What's going on?"

"Melissa's pregnant."

CHAPTER 17

what the what?!

WHEN YOUR WIFE IS PREGNANT YOU HAVE TO READ THINGS. Even when pregnancy goes perfectly it's a confusing time for guys, and after you say something like, "Seriously, you're going to eat that too?" your wife might think that some enlightenment on the plight of pregnancy might help. After endless passages of *Girlfriend's Guide to Pregnancy* and *What to Expect When You're Expecting*, I was more confused than before. Tim wasn't much help so I walked in blindly, learning a few survival tips along the way.

If any of you reading this are guys, this chapter is a gift—a heads-up. It's my recognition and reward for you being a guy reading the memoir of another guy. These are the RogNotes© for what the nine months of pregnancy will look like from a guy's perspective.

Okay, so here is the first thing you can expect when she's expecting. Denial. Don't worry, it's normal. You will suppress all thoughts of fatherhood and will only be reminded that your wife is pregnant when she starts acting crazy. Like, crazy crazy. Again, don't worry; it doesn't last forever. I'm referring to the denial. When this thing called pregnancy starts taking over the woman known as your wife, the denial will mature into avoidance.

Though I'm not a clinically trained expert on the subject, here is the difference between the two. Denial is the blissful lack of reality graciously bestowed upon the male species as a coping mechanism during the crazy transition of becoming a father. It is a gift from God. When reality eventually sinks in, avoidance is the ability to recognize the metamorphic transition you are going through, and then completely ignore it. It is a gift from Anheuser-Busch.

Though it's not all bad. If you are one of the lucky ones, for a while the sex is really good. Now that it's a foregone conclusion, all caution is thrown to the wind and you're like a couple of virgins on the *Titanic*. Her body begins to change. The initial changes work to your favor. Something happens with her breasts. I don't know why it happens—I didn't get that far in those books—but it's great. Take advantage of it. Eventually there'll be competition.

These are the good months, the first trimester. In time, as the baby grows inside her you will begin to wonder if sex is such a good idea. At some point you will have a thought. You will wonder if it is possible—if it can be true. You will be embarrassed to ask because you think you should know these things, so you will go on wondering, full of curiosity and guilt. Then one morning or afternoon or night when your wife gives you the go-ahead signal, the green light, the "All systems are go," you will hesitate, hem and haw, and be made suddenly impotent by the thought, *What if I poke the baby?* So instead you will offer to go buy some mint-chocolate-chip ice cream.

This is the transition into the next phase of pregnancy: the food phase. In other circles it's known as the second trimester. It is also good. All the food you had to sneak out to eat only a few months back is now piled in your refrigerator and pantry, stacked like salty, fat-laden, vinegary heaps of treasure, continually restocked from the late-night cravings of your formerly organic wife. You will gain what is known in the business as "sympathy pounds." It's totally legit; embrace it. Months go by, pounds go on, and soon you are placing the remote control on your wife's baby-filled belly, conveniently located next to you like a side table, as you are watching reruns of *Friends*. She will be crying. Then all of a sudden the remote control will get kicked off her belly.

This is the announcement of the third phase. For those of you still figuring out the pattern, it's the third trimester. It's the *Alien* phase. And it's a little freaky. It starts subtly, with the baby's kicks your wife will feel inside her belly. She will ask you if you can feel it. Just say yes. It's better for everyone that way. Then eventually you do feel it. It's your first physical contact with the kid, and it is exciting and wonderful and you look at your wife and there are tears and you wish you could describe the way you feel without sounding like a metaphysical Mathew McConaughey, but you can't so you just give in and drawl, "Dude, it's sooo awesome."

But then you *see* it move. It looks like something crawling under your wife's tightly stretched skin. Like a baby badger. It's crawling for a moment below the surface, pressing against the outside world, sensing danger then retracting to safety. Everybody wants to touch the badger. Other women. Other women's husbands. Strangers feel up your wife's belly in public and you think that maybe you should punch them but realize there's a societal hall pass on feeling up the bellies of pregnant women so you keep an eye on things, just to make sure it doesn't get too rowdy.

Everything changes for me when we find out it's a boy. It's no longer an "it"; it's a son. He grows and the kicking gets stronger and more visible, and since we're an adaptive species I get used to it. We play games. I get a little soccer ball and balance it near the naval and encourage my future Beckham to bend it off the belly. I start the lessons, giving my protégé a competitive edge, a little advantage for his first AYSO soccer team. No swarm ball here. My son has skills. He's constantly kicking, and it's all fun and games until Melissa reminds me that the baby is due in a few weeks and I need to get the room ready.

I've had eight months and still haven't done anything with it. I'm already a slacker dad. I'm not ready. I'm not qualified. The doubts are set on autodial, calling at all times of the night, and I slip back into denial and avoidance. Painting the room helps. While I'm in here I could be painting anything. I could be painting my man cave. It's baby blue.

It's a summer day and is business as usual. I'm going to work and talking about the storms coming in and hoping they don't knock out the power. The day is going as routine as iced lattes and Chinese take-out and then I get the call from my wife. It's time. Time for what? . . . Oh, for that? Now we are here in the delivery room and the final phase of the male pregnancy begins. Acceptance. I look around the room and say to myself, "Wow, it looks like this is really going to happen," as if there were still some question about it.

While Melissa is getting prepped and hooked up to things, I buckle down and start cramming for the father test. When the moment arrives I volunteer to hold her hand and be the team cheerleader, reciting all those helpful cheers we learned in breathing class. I'm trying not to look down there. Trying to keep things focused on the upper regions. Then someone pulls out a mirror.

"Good God!"

There is a machine near her head that seems important so I put myself in charge of reading it.

"You're doing great," I say. "Your vitals are looking good," I encourage. "Keep breathing," I instruct.

She wants to know if everything is okay.

"Everything is good. You look great."

She looks like she's about to die. I'm getting concerned that I will have to raise this boy on my own.

There is a flurry of excitement. The nurses are talking in code. Something is happening in the mirror. Something is coming out. Something with mucous and blood. Something from the *Alien* movie.

"What the what?!"

I look away before my eyes burn.

"Your vitals are still great," I encourage. "Keep breathing," I instruct.

There's pushing and panting and nurses smiling and the doctor is calling plays.

"Hey, dad, come down here."

"That's okay. I'm cool up here."

"Come down. Don't you want to cut the cord?"

"No. No I don't."

He doesn't believe me.

"Here, cut the cord."

He grabs me and puts some scissors in my hands. They're weighty. They feel nice. I would like to have a pair.

"Cut here. Between the clamps."

"Where?"

"Between the clamps."

I wonder if he needs me to do it closer to one clamp or the other. I don't know how much he needs to tie off the end like a water balloon.

"Here?"

"Yes, between the clamps."

I do it. It feels a little like cutting a bicycle tube. Or a squid.

"Congratulations! You're a dad."

And just like that, I'm a dad.

They wipe all the whatever off it and it finally looks like a baby. A baby boy. He cries for the first time and I hold him, giving him the first of a million words of comfort. I look into my wife's dead-tired, beautiful eyes, and like the baby I am reborn. I want to become the man my son deserves. I want to get up early. Read the Bible more. Pray more. Eat less fast food. Teach him to surf. Teach him the perfect backcast. Help him with his homework. Help him with his college admissions. Help him with job applications. I want us to build a cabin together in the woods. Nail by nail, log by log. I want to be wise for him. Adventurous for him. Safe for him. I want to live with courage and give him every confidence I never had. I want to be his dad. Always.

Things quiet down. Soon Melissa is taking a well-deserved nap and it's just me and the baby. All the cramming for the father test has made me confident. I'm praying for him and speaking in fatherly tones about his destiny. I'm doing great. There is a Bible nearby so I start reading out of Proverbs, filling him with wisdom and truth. I'm the best dad this world has ever seen. Then this newborn bundle of love makes what we new parents refer to as a "poo-poo." I look around for a shovel. Not finding one, I look over to my wife and wonder if I should wake her. I look for a nurse.

"Black stuff just came out of my baby's butt."

She says that it's normal. I want to see her credentials. She then reminds me that I'm the father, I can figure it out. I look at my son who doesn't seem bothered at all by the black alien goo.

"Okay. We're going to do this mano-a-mano."

I figure it out. All the crevices are clean, the aliens have been properly disposed of, and the world is back to normal. I'm amazing. I'm Superdad. Then he begins to cry, so I wake her up.

We are back home and baby is in his newly painted room and the baby gates are in place and there are safety locks on all cupboards containing sharp or poisonous items. All electrical sockets have been blocked, and things are going perfectly when we run out of diapers. Melissa sends me out to get things for the baby.

"What does he need?"

"You're the dad, figure it out."

After several hours I come back with diapers and a child's fishing pole. She looks at me with dread, realizing she may have to raise two children.

CHAPTER 18

Jesus has left the building

IN MY OPINION, SUMMER IN THE SOUTH IS AN AFFLICTION. It makes me melt. I feel like a melting statue of butter. A lumpy and molten statue with sweaty crevices. It's horrible for me, and it's horrible for anybody who has to see me. So when vacation came, we headed to California to cool off on the beach and attend a family reunion at the lake cabin.

To get there we drove through the southern San Joaquin Valley, which was long and hot and filled with memory. Just north of Bakersfield I exited the 99 to show Melissa the house where I used to live. Pulling into the cul-de-sac, I noticed the tree we planted in the front yard was full grown. Also that no kids were running down sidewalks playing kick the can. There were no signs of life.

Everything else about the house looked the same, only smaller. I showed her the neighborhood where I delivered newspapers and the high school entrance where I walked on stilts and drove her to the Sumps only to find them covered with new homes. I wondered how they could have built foundations over sinking tar pits. The scene reminded me of a sad story I read long ago and through the graces of time forgot.

There was a definitive moment of arrival on the drive to the cabin. It was when we crested the top of the last hill and entered into the canopy of ponderosa pines surrounding the lake. It was a gateway, a time portal where past and future lounged lazily with the present. Here lakeside summer shorelines filled with aluminum fold-up chairs with rusted bolts and nylon straps, their various stages of unraveling imprinting checkered patterns in the sensitive skin of sunburned backs. Upon entering there was an associated reflex of rolling down the window and taking the first breath of mountain air. The temperature dropped ten degrees.

There were sounds of birds and boats, and there was a waterfall and kids were screaming and splashing, and parents were yelling for them to be careful as they ran to build speed for perfect cannonballs off wooden docks into the cool blues and greens of lake water below. The purity of air cleansed the soul from pollution of the valleys. Childhood scenes danced softly along the back of scented pines, traveling from the forests of my youth to the memory banks of the man I had become in their shade.

My grandpa had arrived early to ready the cabin. He was always early. We once had a meeting scheduled for a specific time, and I thought I would impress him by showing up fifteen minutes early. I was still fifteen minutes late. So when we got to the cabin he was already there, but he was not getting the boat ready or working on the motorcycles or blowing away those pinecone droppings that collected on the path between the deck and the dock and pricked the bottom of your feet like a bee sting. He was resting. But the lake was blue and calling, so we put on our swimsuits and jumped in.

A little later I found Grandpa sitting alone at the edge of the deck looking over the lake. He had started coming here in his twenties. First camping on the other side of the lake and upgrading from tents to trailers to cabins. Fifty years and a lifetime later, now sitting on a deck of a cabin filled with kids, grandkids, and great grandkids, he was quietly sitting, quietly watching, quietly fulfilled.

I loved these moments with Grandpa. He was always going, always fixing, always inciting, always exploring, always solving. So these moments were rare treats. I grabbed a soda and pulled a chair next to him. On the other side of the large picture-frame window of the cabin's living room I was sure my grandma was watching. She was always watching. She measured my growth over the years by how tall I was as I sat next to Grandpa at the end of the deck. My head came to his elbow and then his shoulder and then his head and eventually maybe an inch or two higher. But I still felt small next to him.

As I sat he smiled and asked how I was doing. Work, marriage, life. Doing good, doing good, doing good. Life was good. In fact it was great. I was finally on top. I finished my checklist of good things in my life and asked how he was doing. He paused, looked at me, back at the lake, and told me: "I have cancer."

It didn't register so he told me again. I didn't have a response mechanism for this so I asked all the questions I'd seen on TV or in the movies. Questions like, "Are you sure?" and "What kind is it?" and "How long do you have?" Turns out cancer is more complex than that. It's a sophisticated killer. Cancer likes to play chess. You make a move and it makes a countermove. It's thinking three moves ahead, planning a counter to your countermove before you make it.

Grandpa patiently listened to my questions. He tried to cheer me up by saying it wasn't contagious and moved on to the next subject. I went back to trying to swim and trying to fish and trying to figure out what to do while dark clouds gathered over the lake.

Grandpa was as timeless and sturdy as the trees surrounding us. In my mind he had no beginning, and until then I had never thought of him not being there. I am the son of his son, and much of who I am can be traced to who he was. He taught me to water-ski on this lake. He taught me to ride a motorcycle along its shore, and as I grew older we rode deeper and higher into the mountains, over passes and ridges until we reached their peaks and all the world lay before us.

On a ride the summer after I turned twenty-one, we stopped at the Jones General Store, operating in a building still standing since the early 1900s. It was a simple country store at the edge of an alpine meadow. The red paint of the wood siding had long faded and the tin roof extended over a covered porch the entire length of the store. Grandpa got a couple of old-fashioned root beers he loved to wash down an Abba-Zaba candy bar with, and we sat in rickety rocking chairs on the porch looking over the green and yellow grasses of the meadow.

Until that time we never talked much about Dad. I wasn't ready, and maybe he wasn't either. I only knew my dad after the drugs but wanted to know more about him before they took over his life. Over root beers and candy bars, Grandpa told me stories of Dad's life I had never heard. At the end of those stories, I asked if he still believed in God after all that happened. He told me that he believed even more because of it. He said there was an evil in this world that closed in around Dad. In this world, Dad suffered beyond measure. Beyond this world, he was finally at peace. Someday we all will be.

———————

Back in Ventura, I called Tim. He could immediately sense something was wrong and dropped what he was doing to meet me over coffee. When I told him about Grandpa, he was devastated. He understood.

Over time I've found life to be impossibly difficult to navigate without a dad, so I built a replacement team. Kind of a "team Dad." It included Tim, my mom, various mentors, various books and magazines, various guys behind the counters of fishing stores, and, of course, Grandpa, who was the unofficial coach of team Dad. Without Grandpa the team would fall apart. Nobody else knew the plays.

"Are you going to stay in Nashville?"

"I'm not sure. I have so much going on out there."

"Is any of that more important than what's going on here?"

Tim asked more questions and gave me space to think and answer each one before asking the next. He listened long enough for me to start sorting out my problems, and as he talked I realized Tim was stepping in as assistant coach and had some plays of his own.

The conversation switched from cancer and death, and we talked about our boys. He'd been a father a couple of years longer than me, which made him an expert. Or so he thought. We talked through my fatherhood fears. "I don't know what I'm doing." "I'm afraid." "What if I break the baby or lose it like a sock?" I confessed my doubts one by one as if he were a priest on the other side of a veil created from the steam of our coffees.

Tim caught me up on his life. Being a father was great, but he was struggling to balance marriage and work and ministry. There was not enough time for it all, and his wife kept falling down the priority ladder. Even further down was the list of things she kept asking him to fix around the house. He had time for anybody in need of help but didn't have time to fix the screen door. As a result, their marriage was strained.

Though he was struggling, I could see he was also coming into his own. He seemed more solid, denser in quality. As we sat, there was a constant flow of people saying hi to him before getting their coffees. With coffee in hand, they stood above us to get his attention before leaving. I didn't know these people, so as each of them stopped, Tim introduced us, and when they left he gave me a little background.

There were no good-byes. It's as if he was in midstream of a hundred conversations, and with each he seemed to elevate it to a next level. He introduced me to Jason who was also a regular at the coffee shop. I remembered him from before I left for Nashville, and while I'd been gone he had gone through a messy divorce involving kids and his world was crumbling. These conversations with Tim slowed the decline.

Before leaving, Tim showed me his new motorcycle. For as long as I'd known him he'd wanted a Harley. Tim always loved motorcycles, and he and his dad started a side business buying old bikes, fixing them up, and selling them for a profit, though he was more interested in riding than selling. Through the process he was able to get a Harley Davidson FXDX and trick it out in black and chrome.

They were recently riding together when his dad got pulled over, and as Tim laughed to himself he got pulled over too. In a father-and-son bonding moment, they went to traffic school together and were forced to tell jokes in front of the class in order to leave. Motorcycles were a way for them to connect, and they were making up for lost time. Tim became a spiritual mentor to his father. At one point his father came to him and in serenity confessed, "I get it about God."

Tim smiled.

"Finally."

When I got back to Nashville, Tim and I talked even more over the phone. It reminded me of school when we talked for hours about how to handle issues with girls or their boyfriends or to help each other with geometry and Spanish. Or when I called him from my college dorm to talk about how much harder the homework was there or to work out details of an upcoming gig or run by the lyrics of a new song or to describe how beautiful the girl was I'd just met from Auburn. He'd say he stopped there once coming back from Tahoe, which led to talking about snowboarding and surfing, and I'd forget about the homework and girls and just be happy to be talking with Tim.

Life became more difficult. Things got harder. There were babies crying in the background. I needed to make a decision. I needed Tim to help me think through this decision. On the other end of the line, on the other side of the country, thank God, he was there.

There was big buzz in Nashville when *Passion of the Christ* released in theaters. The buzz was partially about the movie but mostly about how Hollywood stars were coming to town to drum up interest in the movie. You never knew where you might see Mel Gibson or the guy who played Jesus. Rumors of Jesus sightings spread through town more quickly than when the "Nun Bun" came out of the oven at the Bongo Java coffee shop. Nashville was being discovered. It was full of promise and potential.

I was in the middle of something special, the right opportunity at the right time, and there was no limit to how far it could go. Even after the movie came back to Nashville, I thought maybe there was some meaning to it. Maybe Jesus was moving here. Maybe he would live down the street, hopefully not in that gated community, and we would see each other at the bookstore or Starbucks and start up a conversation and talk about the goings-on around Nashville. And then he would tell me if I was supposed to stay here to keep pursuing my dream or go home. He would know.

I had a big trip coming up. Through a relationship with my boss I had recently met the president to discuss what we were doing at Rocketown. He was thoughtful and sincere and asked questions that made me nervous. Not because they were difficult or self-revealing but because they were asked by the president of the United States, and there were guys with guns close by. He liked our answers, and now we were going to the White House for a follow-up meeting.

The White House looks bigger on TV. I was wearing my best and only suit, standing in the rose garden, looking a few yards over to the entrance where I've watched foreign dignitaries exit in their vehicles on the nighttime news. There was nothing between me and the front door of the White House. I was supposed to be meeting Kathy, the special assistant to the president, but I couldn't remember if I was supposed to meet her at the security gate or actually in the White House.

As I was calling to confirm, some Japanese tourist on the other side of the fence took pictures of me, so I pretended to be negotiating international diplomacy when she answered the phone. I was supposed to meet her in the West Wing. Of course. At the end of the meeting Kathy extended an invite for me to visit any time I'm in town.

I called Tim to tell him about my trip to Washington.

"That sounds awesome."

It was awesome. I began to tell him more about how awesome I was, but then he asked, "How's your grandpa doing?"

And we talked about things that really matter.

There were still no conclusive test results about Grandpa's cancer. Ironically, even though my time at Rocketown had helped me begin the process of letting go of my goals, this detour to Nashville had gotten me closer to them than I could have otherwise imagined. Going home would mean walking away from it all. But the prospect of losing Grandpa made me want to go home and spend as much time with him as I could, whether for a few months or another thirty years.

The skate park was empty so I grabbed my board and climbed to the top of the eight-foot bank. The Rocketown skate park was an echo bouncing off canyon walls of mine and Tim's imaginations. From the top of the bank I could see the whole skate park and could trace every ramp to my friendship with Tim. I dropped in and built speed. The bank was designed like the ones Tim and I found in Orange County.

It was spring break in high school and we loaded up his little red truck with surfboards and skateboards and headed south, radio blasting, arms out the windows, eating at In-N-Out, finding new waves, finding freedom. I raced across the flats and rolled over the pyramid, near ledges similar to those we found on a trip to San Francisco and recreated in Skate Street. The sound of wheels on wood was familiar, soothing. I pumped a few times to build speed for the transition to the vert wall. A mural of Johnny Cash reminded me of where I was and how far I'd come. From the Sumps to Kmart Hill to Skate Street to Nashville to the White House.

I was going fast now, faster than I had in a long time. I was riding by instinct. My feet knew where to go. My back foot cradled the curve of the board between the trucks and tail and my front foot slid back, just a bit, and I rolled forward to the balls of my feet. They were ready. The wall was right in front of me so I bent my knees to absorb the transition of leaving the flat ground to go to vert.

The speed took me up. Higher and higher. At the top I was weightless, my arms stretched wide. Everything was below me. The skate park. The past. The future. I was not thinking of any of it. Up there all there was to think about was flying. Things were clear and I was certain. Suddenly I was back to earth, skating and carving through the memories of every ramp ever built until I ended up in the mini ramp, similar to the first one Tim and I built on top of Kmart Hill so long ago. Skating through the park, I knew what was next. I was going home.

I was on the balcony looking over the skate park when the door burst open.

"You missed it, Roger!"

"What? What did I miss?"

"Jesus was here. He just left the building."

CHAPTER 19

thirty-three

I'VE ALWAYS WONDERED IF I WOULD BE AS BIG AS MY DAD. He's forever fixed in my mind to be two feet taller than me, the distance between a thirteen-year-old and a grown man. He soars in my memories. Even in those with others at the house, smoking, playing records, shooting pool in the garage, he is bigger than them all. Not necessarily taller, but more substantial. They're made of clay. He's made of steel. As an adult I still find myself looking up when I think of him.

Boys grow up physically comparing themselves to their fathers. Each winter they pick up and carry one more log to the fire until one day their dad ceremoniously tells them they are carrying the same size load. On the next trip the boy will try to carry one more. Most boys will grow up to one day realize they are the same size as their dads. Even bigger. To compare yourself to your father is an important part of becoming a man.

Things weren't quite right. We'd moved back to Ventura but it didn't feel like home. On top of that, Dad had been on my mind a lot lately. I'd soon be thirty-three, the same age he was when he died. Like him I had a young family. Like him I had a house and a job, dreams about the future, about what my son would become, about working hard and providing a better life for him. The world was covered in dew. Morning light awakened possibilities I couldn't see.

I couldn't see past this next birthday. Darkness gathered on the horizon with the promise of storms ahead. I'd consulted the map and there was only one way through it, and I didn't want to go, afraid my equipment would break under the strain of the wind. I'd been told this is a common issue with children whose parents passed away young. That it's normal to struggle imagining yourself being older than your parents. They told me I was normal. It didn't help. They said the only way to move forward was to deal with my dad's death. I was frustrated because I thought I had. I'd had counseling. I'd gone to the mountaintops to talk to God.

I realized it was not just the inability to see myself at thirty-three-and-a-half or thirty-four that was bothering me. It was the senselessness of Dad's death. He was so young. I felt so young. Life was just getting started. There was still plenty of time to fix the problems. So I'd gained a little weight. I could go on a diet. So our bank account was low. We could make a budget, start saving. There were relationships that needed repairing. I could call them up. Ask them out to coffee. Apologize.

At thirty-three the world had some cuts and bruises, but the healing power of time was on the side of life. Anything was still possible. Everything was still possible. It was too early to die. I wondered what my relationship would be like with him now. I wondered about what kind of a grandpa he would be. Would he want to be called Papa instead of Grandpa? Would he dress as Santa? Would he teach my son to fish? My dad was robbed of his possibilities. My son was robbed of a grandpa. I was robbed of my dad.

I'd been told several times that Jesus was thirty-three when he died. The first came from a relative shortly after my dad's funeral. They were trying to comfort me by saying since Jesus was the same age as my dad when he died God uniquely understood my suffering. Much later, while I was still suffering, someone took a different pass at it. They said that because there is purpose in everything God does, there was a reason that Jesus was thirty-three. It was enough time to perfectly complete the task given to him. I'm sure I must have asked what Jesus' task was but I can't remember the answer. Though even if I did, it would be constantly changing.

I was surprised by these feelings. I was a man now. I was a dad. But I couldn't help feeling I'd been following some obscure path through the wilderness that had suddenly ended. I could look back and see places where the path had been clear and places where it disappeared and I had to hunt around through the underbrush before finding it again. Though obscure at times, it was there; it had a scent I could find and follow.

But suddenly it was gone. Lost. The trail had ended. From its final edge I could see through a small clearing ending in a dark forest beyond. I knew there were mountains in the distance that required crossing. I knew there were passes and endless meadows and a secret fishing hole on the other side. And I knew there must be a way to get there, but from where I was there was no clue. I searched from present through past, but the only thing recognizable was death, and I saw it everywhere. It was in the forests, below the mountain, around every bend. I couldn't see the trail. I couldn't see past thirty-three. I thought I was going crazy. I needed to talk to someone.

"Hey, Tim, it's Rog."

"Hey. What's up?"

"I'm struggling. I'm thinking about my dad. I'm turning thirty-three, the same age he was when he died."

"I'll be right over."

Tim knew every struggle I'd ever had with my dad. He had a twenty-year log of conversations we'd had on the subject. He had been at every graduation ceremony of my father issues as they passed from junior high to high school to college to single life to marriage, and the ones emerging from this new stage of life. He once again listened and once again ticked off twenty years of reasons why I would cut a new trail. One that was better than any that I could have found or borrowed. One that, when necessary, he would help me to cut. He was confident about it. I knew his confidence came from a combination of talent, luck, BS, and bullheadedness, but in it I found comfort. Tim called on the day of my birthday to see how I was doing. My birthday was fine. It came. It went.

Tim held my history. Like I hold his. It's been defined by the journey of our friendship. An unlikely pairing of a kid with no friends and one with too many. It's been an epic story. A saga. It would be hard to write a script of two friends closer than us. Closer than brothers.

We've written music. We've built businesses. We've built a life and have made promises to each other about how to live them. We've fought off the devils. We've climbed mountaintops to talk with God. We've walked with Jesus. We've explored the West, and when that wasn't far enough we've ventured off to fight in other galaxies. We've beat the odds. We've won the girls. Being fathers was the latest in a lifetime of adventures we had together. It was time to raise sons for the sequel.

―――――――

Tim and I were at Simone's and we were once again talking and dreaming about the future. We'd hung out a number of times but hadn't had the deep reconnection we were both longing for. As I arrived he was writing in his journal with his Bible open next to him. Both were worn. There was a peace about him I hadn't seen in a long time.

He immediately told me the latest thing his son had said. His son was only three but had a vocabulary suggesting he was processing the world differently than other three-year-olds. More mature. More astute. More like his father. He had recently shown me a picture of his son soaring high above his outstretched hands, arms and legs in perfect flying formation, eyes locked onto his father. The more Tim talked about his son the more he swelled. He was a vessel expanding. For the noblest of truths is the unending love a father has for his son.

In becoming fathers we had been transformed. We'd been given new hearts. As a son I could no more know hope than a game of catch with my father. Yet each day I waited. And with each day came a spark of hope, fueled by the kindling of a young heart. But the embers extinguished and the forests of my heart burned out until all that remained was charred earth and the black soot of fire. However, the heart of a father sees further. Further than the limits of this earth. Past the darkness and through the night, to golden shores and the swift light of dawn. In a father's heart is embedded a hope, great enough to believe any prodigal will return.

Changing the subject, I asked, "How are things with Miki?"

He shifted in his chair like he had a great secret to share. Something had changed. He talked about her like he did when they were dating. He went on to say how much fun they were having and how hot she was and I thought maybe I should leave so he could call her and they could get a room. They'd come to some new place. They were more in love. They were happy. They'd become one. He was excited to tell me they were trying for their second child. He liked the trying part. The fact she'd put up with him all these years was a miracle. She had made him into something better. And he finally knew it.

We headed to Skate Street to discuss what was next. He had torn the ramps up to get ready for the third version, and it was eerie to walk into an empty skate park. For the third act he wanted to recapture the innovation of the first and add the things we'd learned from both versions of Skate Street as well as Rocketown. It would once again be the pairing of our imaginations. Like seeing someone you love after being away for a long while, the feeling came back.

I finally felt like I was home.

I had to leave for a short trip so we made plans to get together in a few days to outline the third act of our vision. Tim was going to put a few things together for us to review when I got back. It was a warm spring day so he decided to ride his Harley to work. He had on a leather jacket and black low-top Converses, and he rode with a cool confidence. You would almost expect the scene to play in black and white. The day was routine with people and meetings and progress reports, and daylight was fading so it was time to head home. The world was an open road. He was riding home in the sunset to throw his son in the air and make love with his beautiful wife.

While on my trip I was expecting a phone call from Tim, but Dan kept calling instead. We met Dan while launching our first clothing company. He became a sales rep for us and grew to be such a dedicated friend that he took the whole ride with us. Dan was running the off-site events so I figured he had a question about that.

"Hey, Dan. How's it going?"

There was only silence.

"Dan?"

"I don't know how to tell you this, Rog. Tim just died."

He had just turned thirty-three.

CHAPTER 20

the theater

Three Days Until Memorial

I WAS LOOKING FOR GOD BUT I COULDN'T FIND HIM. I was calling out, yelling, pleading. He was not there. He was on vacation or taking a coffee break or was tied up in a meeting with more important people. I left another message. It was urgent. I was alone. I was standing on the edge of a cliff, above the beach where Tim and I once worked. I'd just flown home and my eyes were swollen, bloodshot, and blurry. Heart was racing. Blood was pumping. I was asking God to reveal himself. He was a no-show. He was hiding. He was a coward.

My head filled with four-letter words of desperation. They came unannounced, indiscriminate of my surroundings, raw as grief. They were in rhythm with my fist, knuckles scraped and bloody from the punching. Punching the dash, punching the empty passenger's chair, punching the No Parking sign. Punching anything else I stumbled into.

With every punch the words came. They came from everywhere and nowhere. There were no others. They filled the space between my thoughts, and when thoughts fled, they filled the emptiness. For when the world fails, the words go with it, until every word ever spoken is reduced to guttural utterances. They were sounds of hopeless despair. A sinking ship. They created the vortex I was desperately swimming against as everything around me was sucked into a dark, bottomless sea.

I couldn't control the crying or the heaving, and between labored breaths the words still came. The further I sank, the louder I screamed, until the sucking noise drowned my voice and all I could do was motion the word *Jesus* on my lips, the last *s* hanging on the crevice of a mouth dried from the screaming. I could see up through the vortex a world cresting as a rogue wave, crumbling down, building speed and momentum, crushing me into the lowest depths of the ocean. The last thing I saw before disappearing into darkness was the end of a rope, edges frayed from use.

The phone rang. It was Dan again. He was overcome with a feeling he needed to call me back. I found a picnic bench a few steps back from the ledge and sat on top of the table, legs still twitching from the adrenaline. He was talking and talking and I was wondering what this had to do with anything. Tim was dead. What was there to talk about? He wanted to know things. He wanted to hear me say I was okay, that I wasn't doing anything stupid. He wanted to know where I was at that moment and where I would be the next. He wanted to know if I was okay to drive or if he should pick me up. He wanted to know what I was going to say.

"Say about what?"

"Rog, you've been friends with him longer than anybody. People will be looking to you. You will need to say something at the funeral. What are you going to say?"

Two Days Until Memorial

There was a gathering to make plans. It felt like someone should be in charge. Someone older and more experienced with these sorts of things. Maybe they should have had some gray hair and worn a buttoned-up shirt with a soft jacket so when they pulled you close to say that everything would be okay, you would feel comforted and you would believe it. They would have glasses but take them off when they talked to you, removing any barriers between you and the empathy emanating from their eyes. I kept looking around the room for this person but he was not there. We were the grown-ups. This grief was ours.

Grief became pandemic. It was in my blood and my wrists were slashed. With each pulse I was bleeding over anybody who came near. People came with all forms of Band-Aids. Emotional. Spiritual. They told me God must have a purpose for taking Tim. They told me God loved Tim even more than we did. They said Tim must have been pretty amazing for God to want to take him home early. They told me about the bright side. There was one more angel in heaven. Tim was in a better place now. Condolences were given like secondhand roses.

I took my journal to the beach and pulled a pen from my bag. It was a pen Tim gave me. I used it to try and write something for his memorial, but the town was filled with ghosts. I was sitting under palm trees at the Point, looking north to Hobo Jungle, and Tim and I were paddling out into the ocean with surfboards we shaped in the Skate Street garage. It was an El Niño year with water unseasonably warm, so we were still trunking it in October. We both agreed it was the best surf session we'd had there. The sun was rising and I was paddling toward it, the ocean bringing me this gift, this pulse of energy coming from a southern-hemisphere storm, traveling all this way so that for a moment I could be in union with the universe.

Tim was watching as I dropped in. I was stroking my arms into the water, digging deep and furious, each arm alternately extending, reaching for the bottom of the ocean where at my furthest reach fingers curled and grabbed at the water, trying to hold it and bring it to the surface. I was building speed, and now the ocean was working with me. We were in unison. It wanted to give as much as I wanted to receive. The pulse of energy that had traveled thousands of miles was taking shape. The contours of the ocean floor pushed it up, and behind me the wave built. Taller and taller until it could no longer support its own weight. It curled forward, its fingers reaching toward its wrist, holding me in the palm of its hand. In this curl I was safe, the wave opening in front of me. With a slight adjustment of weight, a pushing of rail into the water, I was floating down the wave effortlessly, weightless and free.

As I paddled back Tim was smiling, the first light of morning warming his face. He was saying something. What was it? I could see him there. He had a message for me. He said something I promised never to forget. I was trying to hold on but memories of Tim were already fading. Desperately I tried to bring it back. If I lost this memory, what else would I lose? How long could I hold on? How long? Almost, almost, it was gone. He was gone. A ghost blown by the wind, back into the ocean from which it came.

One Day Until Memorial

I couldn't sleep. I woke in the gray, between darkness and light, and in a brief, hopeful moment thought it had been a dream. But realizing I was awake, death again played a relentless game of racquetball in my stomach. Light soon cast its first shadows, and in the mid-consciousness of early morning I grabbed my journal from the previous day and continued to write. I didn't know what to write and wanted someone to come and move my wrist for me. I looked for God and again couldn't see him. I'd been abandoned, forsaken. I felt alone.

The thoughts were jumbled and scattered, and I couldn't will them into place. I was trying to wrestle them down and pin their shoulders to a blank page, and the page was taunting me, daring me to try and come up with a single word that could adequately describe my friendship with Tim. I couldn't do it. It was impossible. I couldn't have done it in a million words. I didn't want to start because as soon as our stories appeared on paper they would become our history. It was not yet day and the world was silent. Then somehow they came. Words appeared on the page. Words whispered through the gray. Some of the words I recognized as my own. As I wrote, he was with me.

Morning of Memorial

Before the public viewing, the funeral home was open to family and a few friends. As I walked in, the air was completely still, so still if I stayed in one place I might have suffocated. I moved slowly. I was the only person in the room, and in the front was a large, elegant wooden box, surrounded by flowers. The front of the box was open, and in the box I could see Tim lying on the silk lining with his arms folded. Only the box lid by his head was open.

The last person I saw lying like this was my dad, and suddenly I was in two places at once. I wasn't sure where to sit. Pull a chair to the casket? Sit a couple rows back? I'd never been so uncomfortable with Tim. He was wearing his favorite black shirt with the cuffs folded back. He looked good but not quite himself. His hair was coiffed. But that wasn't it. Something was missing.

I sat in the front pew to talk to him from a distance. I was afraid to go any closer. I wanted to say something profound. We'd been best friends for so long that I couldn't remember my life without him. I felt as if what I said in that moment would forever seal our friendship. This was my last chance ever to say something to his face.

I wanted to tell him my life was owed to his, that so much of who I am was a result of his friendship. I wanted to thank him for the countless hours he'd listened and for the countless things we'd built. I wanted to say something meaningful, to bring closure to our friendship. I was having trouble thinking of anything to say. I stared into nothing and eventually looked back toward the casket.

"Sorry I never returned your sander."

" . . ."

"It worked nice."

" . . ."

When you've cried and cried and your eyes can produce no more tears, they begin to come from someplace else. They come from pieces of your heart, broken like jagged stones, and must be pushed from your body. The pain is beyond bearing. You convulse and contort and you try to get them out and you think you might die from the pain. As they come, the anticipation of them leaving your body is even worse. For then, those pieces of your heart spill tearlike to the floor for the world to trample, and you're not sure if your heart will ever work again.

These tears dampened my face as I sat, and the pew as I stood, and the carpet as I walked, and when I got close enough, fell onto Tim, wetting his shirt and his face until it looked like he was crying too.

———————

Unrelenting grief will eventually manifest itself in other forms. It's a shape-shifter. Eventually, it came to us in the form of silliness.

It was the public viewing and we had had enough. Enough of the crying, enough of the grief, enough of those flowers sitting behind Tim's casket silhouetting the outline of his face against a bouquet of perfectly trimmed roses. The flowers had to go. It was during the official viewing, before the cremation, so the funeral home was full of people wanting to get one last look at Tim. My wife and I were sitting up front with Tim's wife and Greg, the pastor, trying to keep it together, as she was hunched over, body trembling from the laughter. She poked me in the side.

"Tell Clint to come over."

"I'm not telling him to come over."

"Tell him to come over. Now. Tell him to move the flowers."

"No, I'm not doing that. Ouch."

"Yes, you are."

I motioned for Clint. He was a few rows back. The room was packed.

"Hey, Clint," I whispered.

She was hunched over, body trembling. She looked grief-stricken but was really trying to keep from bursting into laughter, causing an uncomfortable scene, the widow dressed in black, laughing as her dead husband was on display for a room full of people. I looked to Greg but he was laughing-crying and was of no help. Dutifully, Clint came.

"What's up? Is everything okay?"

Clint would do anything for his friends, and I almost felt guilty. But then she poked me.

"No. It's not. Those flowers need to go."

"Which flowers?"

"Those ones behind Tim."

"Behind the casket?"

"Yes. Those ones. He hated those flowers."

"Okay. Where do you want them?"

She didn't say.

"I don't know. Just move them."

Clint went onto the stage, behind the open casket, and picked up the flowers. He was looking back for direction. I gave him hand signals. Over to the left, I pointed. He walked over. He was trying to not make a scene, mouthing the words so as to not disturb anyone, "Here?"

No, not that far, a little to the right. On the ground. Never mind. Put them over on that other stand. No. Not there. Maybe on the ground. Ouch. My side was bruised from the poking. No. Not there either. How about that stand to the left?

It went on like this for a while.

We knew we shouldn't be doing this. We shouldn't be laughing, carrying on. We were passing notes in the back of class while everybody else was listening to the lecture. But this moment was ours. For all of our suffering we were owed this little indulgence. And we would take it. Take what was ours. So we continued. We imagined Tim in heaven, sides splitting with laughter, saying, "That was a good one. I didn't see it coming." We were pleased with ourselves. Like a third-base coach I was giving hand signals.

No. The other side, I pointed.

The whole room was watching, transfixed. They were wondering where the bouquet of roses would end up. Wondering where the perfect spot was. Where they would finally rest. Where their petals would give a nice aroma and their perfectly trimmed stems and the perfectly trimmed filler flowers would politely suggest order, suggest that things were the way they are supposed to be. The room needed the flowers to be in place. People needed things to be settled. Clint looked to me for more instruction.

"Never mind. Just put it back where it was."

Day of Memorial

I was almost finished with the eulogy, and as I wrote I wished I'd taken time to say these things to Tim while he was still alive. It would have only taken a minute to call him and say, "Your friendship means the world to me," or "Your talent inspires me," or "Thank you," or "I love you." All the minutes that ticked by while I did lesser things were an hourglass of regret. What would I have said if I had known? What should I have said though I didn't?

I wish we had welded together. He was a good welder and offered to teach me and showed me the right welder to buy. My dad was a welder, and I always wanted to learn. Tim started to show me while building Skate Street, but I got distracted. I probably had an important e-mail or voice mail and had to walk out to take the call. I can't remember who from. Before we started welding we would have gotten coffee to talk about what we wanted to build, and probably about surfing, and maybe we would even revisit the hypothetical scenario of how we could run for mayor of Ventura together. Neither of us really wanted to do it, but something had to be done about the parking structure on the beach.

I don't know why it takes a funeral to say the things we really feel about each other. It's like eating cake at the dentist. I bought the welder. It's red and has knobs he was going to explain to me. It's sitting in the garage with other tools we bought together, a dusty pile of good intentions.

I was at the beach finishing a section of the eulogy about Tim's son and suddenly I was a child again, standing at the edge of the lake. It was twilight and the fish were jumping. It was late in the season and the evening was cool and the lake was calm. Right in front of me they were jumping everywhere. My heart skipped a beat. I knew that I could catch one this time. Every time I heard a slap on the water, my neck instinctively snapped my head in that direction.

I had my blue tackle box open, and I was looking for something— something special. The guy at the store said if I used this lure that I could catch a trout. They'd been catching them all over the lake on these lures. All you had to do was cast it far enough to where the fish were and slowly reel it in, and *bam*. You'd catch a fish.

I'd bought the lure and put it in the bottom of the tackle box. Nervously I was looking for it. There it was. My heart continued to race as I tied it on. *Slap-slap*. That was a big one. The rings spread on the surface of the water like a bull's-eye. Did I remember how to tie that knot Dad showed me? I was uneasy, worried I'd forgotten. I was tying the knot and hoping it would hold. What if the fish was too big? What if it was so big it took me all night to reel it in? My heart raced at the thought of it. That would make Mom happy, to see me with such a big fish. Finally. I had the perfect lure tied. I remembered the knot. I stepped up to the water's edge to cast.

Slap-slap-slap. Fish were everywhere. Right out in front of me. I made a cast. It wasn't far enough so I reeled it in. I made another cast. Still not far enough so I reeled it in as fast as I could. It was a race against time. *Slap-slap. Slap-slap*. I didn't know how long they would be there so I was working as fast as I could. Another cast. And another. And another. I couldn't cast it that far. If I could just get it out far enough, I'd catch a trout. It would be big, like the ones in the fish case at the grocery store.

I wound up and heaved the lure. Still not far enough. I needed to get it further. I was getting frantic. How long would the fish be there? Dad could cast that far. Easily. He could cast it out there and hand me the pole to reel in the lure and catch that fish. That huge trout. I turned to look for him. He'd be down any moment. He promised. I waited. He wasn't there. He was never coming again. He was dead.

I wound up for the biggest cast I'd ever made. The tip of my fishing pole was straight behind me. The lure was hanging perfectly off the end. My little arms were full of adrenaline. Everything was perfect, just like he taught me. In perfect form I cast the line. The lure was traveling higher, farther than ever before. It was as far as I'd ever cast, as far as I could cast. My heart soared with the lure, arcing in the twilight. It fell short. I couldn't cast far enough to reach the fish. *Slap-slap-slap*. They were out there past my line. Past my reach. I couldn't catch the fish. I slumped down to sit in the sand along the shore, my heart with my lure, sinking to the bottom of the lake.

Slap-slap.

It was the sound of tears rolling off my cold cheek, onto the puddle they'd created on the eulogy below.

CHAPTER 21

eulogy

At the Memorial

I WAS TAKING ONE LAST LOOK IN THE MIRROR TO MAKE sure my suit looked okay, and trying to understand who I was. The way I felt on the inside didn't match what I was seeing in the mirror. Every morning we wake up to put on clothes for the day, and we wear those clothes to work or birthday parties or Christmas or soccer games, and one day you wake up to put on a black suit to deliver a eulogy to your best friend's funeral, and you're wondering how your pants got so tight. Life sometimes feels like a dress rehearsal for a play that got canceled.

Melissa and my job was to get Tim's wife secretly to the memorial, and I couldn't help but feel like we were delivering a celebrity to an awards show. Since the crash people had been hounding her, holding on and smothering, as if she were a portal to the afterlife. Through it all she had been steadfast and courageous. She had held with great poise and patience as others came to deliver their condolences, only seeking to be reassured themselves. For those of us around her, she had been heroic.

On the other end of the spectrum, I'd been selfish. The last few days I'd been absorbed in the pain of Tim's death as if I owned the exclusive license for it. I never stopped to think the pain might be bigger than me. As we pulled up to the Ventura Theater, a line was wrapped around the block. It was full of people. It was full of pain.

The pain had become a shared experience of an entire city. They had all come to experience, one last time, or for the first time, the remnant of a life wonderfully lived. We were collectively, beautifully bound by pain. Mine was just one story in a thousand of how a life was shaped by knowing Tim. The people waiting in line could each write their own story and each would be true and each would be beautiful.

Inside the theater the air was electric with an invisible presence. The air felt pregnant. Heavy. Messy as love. The presence grew denser with each person. They drew it in and it multiplied. The theater could no longer contain it, and it spilled out of the openings and into the street, covering downtown, and soon the entire city. For a minute I forgot where I was. Old friends were coming up to say hello. I was nervous and a little freaked out. I needed to concentrate and rehearse, but they wanted to hear about what I was doing these days.

"Oh, not much. Just moved back to town. Married. Have a son. Another on the way. Working. Tim died so I had to write his eulogy. What have you been up to?"

Eventually they asked, "How are you doing?"

As I was talking my hands didn't know what to do. They were beyond my control. Flailing, wringing, going in my pockets, then out of my pockets, behind my back, on my hips in the power-suit position, holding back my coat jacket just so, revealing the power tie, back in pockets, out again, buttoning jacket closed, pointing in the general direction of Nashville. It's a game of charades. Three words to guess how I'm doing.

"I am fine."

I was not fine. In a few moments I needed to speak to this crowd. Nerves were wreaking havoc on my body, and if I didn't get to a bathroom soon there would be trouble. No more time. The lights were dimming, and the crowd was finding their seats. Backstage I found a door to the alley and stepped out for some air. Someone saw me and asked how I was doing.

"I am fine."

I heard music in the background. My mind was going blank. I was losing it.

I wanted to run, but the presence reached out of the theater and surrounded me in the alley. I was swallowed by it, swimming deep in its beauty. It was almost visible, calling me inside like the scent from hot apple pie on the kitchen window ledge. I turned to the backstage entry; its doors were flung open like arms. There was a soft glow of light emanating from within, and beyond the light was music.

It was as if every favorite song and every song I wrote with Tim had been squeezed into this melody, and I was drawn back. Drawn into the light. Drawn into the music. There were a thousand people singing, and I was swept into the melody. I pulled the eulogy from my coat pocket to review one more time and then joined the chorus.

It was time to give the eulogy.

I stepped into the mic and the theater was silent.

I looked into the light.

I was ready.

Thank you for allowing me the honor of sharing a bit about Tim today. I've had the privilege of being Tim's closest friend for over twenty years. For much of my life I didn't have the name Roger. I was known only as Tim-and-Rog. Even when Tim wasn't around people would look at me and ask, "Hey, Tim-and-Rog. Where's Tim?"

I got to know Tim the same way a lot of you did. I was new, had a bit of a troubled past, and didn't have many friends. He made time for me. Twenty years later he still did. No matter where I was or what time it was, the thing that I always knew is that Tim would be anywhere I asked, moments after I asked it.

When the reporter came to do the story on Tim, there were several of us around telling stories of his life and how he lived it. We talked about his family, his friends, and his community. Well, except for Greg, who talked about him growing up on ranches and in igloos. I found it funny that the only person in the room not telling the truth was the pastor. But the more we got into it, the more it seemed like the story couldn't be true. How can a single person be so talented and have accomplished so much in life? How can a single person touch the lives of so many people? It just doesn't seem possible, but it's Tim.

Over the past few days, as I've been thinking through stories of Tim, it's interesting to see the ones that have stood out. It's not the ones with the huge plots where we talked about faith, marriage, kids, life, death. It's the simple ones where we were just living our lives together.

There was a day in high school when Tim decided we should all dress up in crazy outfits and roller-skate through the school, which incidentally was highly illegal. So we met at his house, as we always did, loaded up in his parents' motor home, and drove up to Buena. As was so often the case, I didn't fully understand what Tim was getting us into until we got there. He was going to fly by some lockers, circle around the principal's office a few times, and pretty much just keep skating until we got caught. Just for the thrill of the chase. It was a great theory, except I had no idea how to roller-skate. But Tim did. And unfortunately he was really good at it (which I can only tell you now because he would have beat me up for telling you). He could do the backward skate, slow, fast, the whole deal. So I just held on to his backpack and let him drag me through it. In fact, a lot of my life was spent this way. I would do my best to grab on to Tim and let him take me where he was going. I always knew he could be trusted to lead the journey, and they were some of the best journeys of my life.

From first meeting in junior high, it seemed every best part of life was done with Tim. We started our band in high school and played through college. And after college we opened our first business together, South Jetty. South Jetty led to Nails and Nails led to Skate Street. Some of my best Skate Street memories with Tim actually were in the period when we had the building, but before we started construction.

Probably one of the worst ideas is to give Tim an empty warehouse full of tools, wood, and heavy industrial equipment. One day when we probably were supposed to be working on something, Tim kept on being distracted by the scissor lifts in the building. So what he thought would be a good and reasonable idea was to have some scissor-lift races—doubles. So I hopped on the back of one and we had one of the best nights of our lives.

Probably the only thing better than screwing around with power tools and heading to Starbucks every fifteen minutes was the time we spent with our mentor Jeff, talking about life and the future, and praying together in the space that would eventually become the vert ramp that launched our business lives.

And it kept getting better.

I want to take the time to thank Tim's family, his parents Lynn and Frank, and his sister Paula, for always believing in Tim. Paula, Tim treasured you as a younger sister, which was evident in the way he brought you around to parties you were too young to be at. Lynn, Tim loved you deeply and often told me how grateful he was to have you as his mom. And, Frank, Tim would always tell me how proud he was of you and how proud he was to be your son. As Tim's parents you should know this room is full of people whose lives were impacted by your son, and we all want to take a moment to honor you and thank you for giving us Tim.

Miki, you are the love of his life. The first moment he told me about you I knew it was trouble. What I didn't realize at the time is what an even better Tim we would have because of you. In fact, the only thing better than Tim was Tim-and-Miki. Miki, you completed him. Thank you for sharing him with us. I know it must have driven you crazy at times to have all the people in your house or to have Tim out walking through life with people instead of fixing your backdoor. This room is also filled because of you. So I also want to take a moment to honor you for the life you lived with Tim. Myself, and everybody in this room, are better people because of you.

And, Gavin Josiah Garrety, I can't wait to tell you stories about your dad and how he sold out the Ventura Theater with all the people who were touched by him. I can't wait to tell you how this community was shaped by the love of your father. And I can't wait to tell you about how your daddy walked with Jesus and how much he wants for you to have that same intimacy. You are your father's son, and we look forward to seeing his legacy continue in you.

Tim knew how to live life, and he got right in thirty-three years what most people take a lifetime to figure out. He lived full of faith, grace, hope, and love. As he begins his next journey, I know his prayer would be for each of us to continue ours in the fullness Jesus has for us.

Thank you, Tim.

I went backstage and collapsed. Utterly spent, but no longer alone.

At the end of the memorial, Greg invited people to come toward the stage as a declaration they'd like to know God the same way Tim did. It seemed the whole theater was on its feet and coming forward, descending in comfortable waves of reassurance that our lives were not in vain. Tim had gone to be with God, and those parts of our hearts connected with his had gone to be with God too. It was a long parade of ascension.

The aisles were full of people, and I was surprised at how few I recognized. Suddenly a face appeared that I remembered. It was Jason, from the coffee shop where Tim liked to hang out. His eyes were still glossy from the tears but his face glowed as someone who may have once been lost, but was now found.

THREE

In Search of What Matters

Thank you, God, for blessing the food to my body at dinner.
And thank you for the trees and the ocean and all the other
things you made. I like all your creations.

—Nighttime prayer of author's youngest son

(at eight years old)

CHAPTER 22

caught inside

I HAD ANOTHER DREAM ABOUT TIM LAST NIGHT. THERE have been many, and they are all versions of the same thing. In these dreams he is happy and assures me he never died. I'm doubtful at first but eventually believe him, and we go on surfing or building something as if nothing had happened and no time had passed. Sometimes we are younger and sometimes we are older. His face is blurred in a way that I don't recognize his features, but recognize an essence of him somehow more real.

In each dream I grasp at the world in which I find him and feel myself reluctantly slipping back to mine. In the complete stillness of the wakening hours, I can sometimes hold onto the feeling a moment longer. It's the one-year anniversary of Tim's death, and some friends will gather to celebrate his life. I don't want to be with friends. I don't want to be with anyone. I go surfing alone instead.

Sunrise comes soft and unnoticed, and the predawn stirs with commercial fishermen, farmers, field laborers, and surfers trolling beaches to find the perfect wave at first light. From the southern boundary, Ventura begins where the Santa Clara River enters the Pacific, near the harbor. The land rises gently, first in plains made rich from topsoil delivered by the river, then rising above, forming foothills to the north where the city slumbers cozily in its reach. Beyond, the hills become mountains with peaks sometimes disappearing into the clouded veil of heaven.

The first light of day is supple, almost bendable. It touches down on the foothills, and on the highest hill are two eucalyptus trees that from town look like oaks. There used to be more, but cruelty of time has reduced them to two. They stand stoically as loyal companions, weathered and worn, from a lifetime of guardianship over our city. In the yellowing of morning, a light breeze stirs the waters of Pierpont Bay.

After lingering in the hillsides, morning light descends upon rooftops of historic buildings downtown. To the east, the city blurs into fields and valleys, farms and orchards, filled with strawberries and row crops and citrus trees with oranges and lemons hanging like ornaments. To the west is the Pacific Ocean, where the sun disappears each evening behind the Channel Islands off our coast. For most of the year, every day comes just as beautiful as the last, with no change of seasons, and soon I am lost in time.

Tim's ashes were scattered in the ocean, and I feel connected to him here. I'm at one of our favorite surf breaks gazing at the water. The ocean, like all of creation, has a certain order to it. Swells are generated by storms over the Pacific, and the quality of the waves is determined largely by how well the swells are organized.

If the storm is close to shore, it doesn't have enough time and space to organize its energy and comes to shore as a total mess. If a storm is thousands of miles in the ocean, originating in Alaska in the winter or around the equator in the summer, there is enough time and distance for the ocean to organize its storm energy into something more manageable, resulting in clean and consistent waves. In the year since Tim's death, the storm has neither time nor distance, and I am still a mess.

If you understand the order of the ocean, you can time swells and determine when the lull occurs between sets of waves, thus paddling out with relative ease. Today I am out of rhythm with the ocean and set out against it on my own timing. There is a place called the impact zone where the force of waves coming is met with the undercurrent of the ocean sucking back, and if you're not careful you can end up getting stuck here, not able to get to the calm outside the breakers or back to the shore.

I'm in the impact zone and can't decide which direction to go. I'm caught inside. It's late spring, the fog is settling, and I barely notice summer. The next season does the same, and soon the years are full of winter. The world continues, but I feel stuck in gray. I find myself withdrawing, disappearing into the fog.

Pain is a mistress beckoning in the silence of night, and I call upon her when every other part of me is numb. I sit or lay or walk in the dark and feel the pain filling me, slowing my steps, slowing my breathing, and the pain pours through my brokenness, filling the fissures and filling the cracks and filling the emptiness until I take a shape nearly resembling my own. I recognize my shadow but no longer recognize myself casting it. Still I cling to the pain. When all other emotion is gone, it is my comfort. For if I can feel pain, perhaps I can once again feel hope or love.

Pain takes the place where Tim once sat, riding shotgun to Solimar and sitting opposite me at a coffee-shop table. It's not nearly enough, but when you're lost in the desert a few drops of water can keep you alive another day. I've created an effigy with the pain, and if it heals I lose that part of him too. It's all that's left. Other than the pain, I feel nothing.

Pain is selfish. It is all consuming. It wants to occupy every inch of my heart and shove out any light so it can be alone in the darkness. I've given in to the self-indulgence of my pain, and nothing around me is as important. People come with words of comfort. They tell me everything I'm feeling is normal. It's what happens when you lose someone.

They assure me I'm normal. They say pain can only be healed with time. That in time the pain will go away. I want to believe them but I know these promises are not true, and I don't think they believe them either. Pain is a poison time cannot heal. It can only dilute. Time is a substance to add to the pain, and with enough you can drink the poison and it may not kill you.

―――――――

I start a new business and open an office downtown and am consumed with life. My second son, who was born a few months after Tim's death, is now four years old and on his sixth surgery. He was born with irreversible nerve damage in his ears and struggles to hear my voice. My wife prays for him to be healed. I try to pray the same but struggle to believe my voice is heard there too. One night while I'm kneeling with him alongside bed for our good-night prayers, in a soft voice he asks,

"Daddy, is God going to make my ears all better?"

I don't know what to tell him.

I've heard preachers talk about how a relationship with God is like a marriage, and if that's true, we need counseling. We get along fine and like to talk about what the kids are up to and the day's events, but when it comes to anything deeper God seems cold and distant. He says he's interested in what's going on in my life, but when I really need him, I can't find him anywhere. The more I don't see him, the more I struggle to trust him. We've grown lukewarm.

I'm not sure our relationship can withstand my doubt, but I stay for fear of life without him. To help with the emotional struggle of all the surgeries, Melissa and I have some friends to our house, and one of them prays for our son to hear God's voice in the silence. Later, I pray the same thing for myself.

Because we're raising two boys, I'm always tired. There's a Starbucks on my way to work where I often stop for coffee to help start the day. I'm in line with a bunch of half-awake customers, looking like precoffee zombies, when I hear the first real words of morning.

"Next customer in line!"

I go through the motions, not sure if I'm getting coffee or am next in line at the airport check-in.

"Grande wet cappuccino."

The barista writes my name on a cup and I wait in another line.

When my drink is ready, I grab my cup and find a seat near others who look as tired as me. We don't talk to each other, but everybody's name is written on coffee cups, like nametags, and we can hear each other's conversations. Mark is on the phone talking about his kids. He's worried about the friends they hang around and isn't sure what to do. David finishes his coffee and leaves his empty cup sitting on the table, again, so the next person has to stand and wonder if anybody is sitting there, and ask the people at the table next to the empty cup if anybody is sitting there, and eventually has to throw away David's cup before sitting at the table.

Jennifer and Debbie are sitting a couple of tables over, talking in voices much too loud, about how unhappy they are with their marriages. Their sex lives just aren't that good anymore. Next to me, Brian is talking to Bob about a surefire property investment, but when Bob declines, Brian changes the subject and discloses he's about to lose everything and doesn't know what to do. A homeless guy weaves through the crowd asking for money, and on his way to the bathroom passes several old guys talking about their prostates, and Alexi-Maximillian who is interviewing for an insurance salesman job.

His interviewer says he'll need to make 300 phone calls per week and of those, should be able to close 1 sale. That's 299 rejections every week. Alexi-Maximillian says he can handle it, but I'm not convinced.

Everybody is suffering. Everybody is uncertain. Everybody is scared. God can be found on the mountaintops, but we need him most in the valleys. Because climbing up is hard, we lop off the mountaintops to fill in the valleys so the pain isn't so deep. As a result, our lives are lived between molehills and ditches, and it can feel as though we're going through the motions, standing in line with the masses until one day we're standing at the gates of heaven, wondering where our lives went, until over the crowd we'll hear, "Next customer in line!"

My new business takes me back to the White House for some meetings, and I bring my grandpa with me. One of my favorite trips with Grandpa was during college. I interned with him, and he took me on a trip to Northern California, where he had to tend to some business. At each business we talked about how it worked, what made it a good or bad business, about the markets they were in, and how he kept track of it all. But in the car we could talk about anything I wanted. I was graduating college soon and didn't know what to do next. Between locations we talked about my dreams and opportunities. By listening and asking questions about what I wanted in life, he helped me through the transition.

I needed him again. Though not at a life transition or crossroad. I needed to know what to do when life unravels at the seams. Like most men of his generation, Grandpa is guarded with his emotions, but he's endured and survived great loss, so I know he can help me. On our trip to DC, between meetings and sightseeing, I laid out my issues about losing Tim and the subsequent fears and confusion. He listened patiently. He affirmed. He encouraged. The trip went well, and on the flight home I mustered the courage to ask something I'd wanted to know for years. Since the birth of my sons I can imagine no greater pain than losing one of them. I asked how my grandpa managed the pain of Dad's suicide.

He stops me from talking any further.

"Is that what you've thought happened this whole time?"

I'm startled by the question. It's been over twenty-five years, and this is what I've always thought. He then goes on to explain my dad didn't take his life; it was taken from him. Grandpa tells me that though the habit was horrible, my dad was smart and knew what he was doing. He got behind with some drug payments. Things got rough. Then Dad was given some drugs mixed with something else that killed him when he used it.

My father didn't choose to leave me. He was taken.

I sat silently, wondering what to do with a world where everything is up for grabs. You can spend a lifetime believing something, wrestling with it, struggling with it, and finally coming to grips with it, only to find out it's something else entirely and you have to start the process all over again. It made me wonder what else might be different than what I first believed. What can we trust? Truth? Love? God? The plane touched down and taxied to our terminal, but I stayed suspended between heaven and earth, not sure if I'd ever land.

———————

Not long after this trip, the stock market collapses. My new business doesn't survive. Until I can figure out what to do next, my grandpa lets me borrow an office already furnished with my grandmother's old desk. The office looks over the junior high I attended, and I spend most of my time staring out the window, to where Tim and I dreamed our dreams and almost made them happen. And I wonder how I'm going to pay the bills.

Most of what we do will be forgotten in our lifetime. The rest will be forgotten shortly after. Tim and I dreamed for years of building a great company that would do great things. We gave years of our lives to this dream. We worked and sacrificed and asked countless others to work and sacrifice and invest, and together we all hammered and welded and painted and prayed and fought about things and didn't sleep and worried and laughed and continued to dream. Then, on the way home from this dream, Tim got hit by a car. In an instant it all became vapor. Soon it will be a good memory for a handful of people. Then it will be gone. I've spent my life building sandcastles at low tide.

I need to know what matters. I need to know how to understand this world and my purpose in it. I've been programmed to build. And I have. Now everything I've built is gone. I've been programmed to dream. And I've dreamed great visions. Now those visions feel like someone else's prescription glasses. Everything is blurry, and I can't see the future. This world is in conflict with itself. It creates beauty only to consume it. It births life only to kill it. There are no happy endings here. Everything in life ends in death. This world's promises are mixed messages of hope and grief. We are made to desire and given our choices. They are the faded flowers of an inglorious beauty.

I've gone downtown to finalize some issues with the closing of my business, and in the shadows of the entryway stands a dangerous-looking man. I feel as though he's watching me. Since my childhood, downtown Ventura has been cleaned up quite a bit, but there is still a dangerous element lingering, and I grow uneasy. I'm scanning my options, but as I approach, the man looks familiar. He's old but looks strong. He has a small, wheeled suitcase, and is standing as if waiting for me. Finally I recognize him as someone I thought long ago dead, and I wonder how it's possible.

"Is your name Bill?"

"Yes. I remember you."

"I used to hang out at the Point all the time. You watched our stuff and made sure we were taken home safely."

Bill has kept up with many of the kids who sat under his watch. He goes on to tell me about what happened to them. I tell him what happened to Tim, but he seems to already know. I find it easy to talk to him and say how much I miss Tim, and he seems to already know that too. I tell him about the business I used to run behind the entryway where he is standing.

He tells me about some of the places he's worked. He'd been a barber and a driver and many other things before I ever met him. Whatever his occupations once were, to me his purpose was far greater. In my most vulnerable summer, every day, there he sat, under the shade of a tree. He asked more questions about my life, and when I finished, he said good-bye and hurriedly wheeled his bag around the corner. I followed and watched as he walked into some low-rent apartments next door to my office.

It turns out Bill wasn't homeless after all.

My mom is a great artist and has more insight into how to see the world than anybody I've ever met. She has painted her entire life and has shown in galleries throughout California. I have spent many hours in her studio and traveling to the galleries showing her work, but I had never painted with her. On a winter's day I ask for a lesson in plein air painting, so we head up into the hills behind Ventura and set up along the road heading to Grant Park. From up here I can see all of Ventura and its beaches, and if I look long enough I can see scenes of my life play out below. But today we're not going to paint everything we see. We're going to focus in on a single view of a tree, and learn to paint it.

I watch my mom set up an easel and pull out her pallet and brushes. She stops and quietly surveys the landscape, and one by one pulls out paints, returning to the landscape between each tube. She instructs me to get my pallet ready with paint, so I pull it out and grab the paint colors to paint the tree and the sky behind it. I grab green and brown and blue and get ready to squirt them on my pallet. Gently, Mom stops me.

"What colors do you see?"

"Green. Brown. Blue."

She instructs me to put the paints away and look more closely. She tells me to study the light.

"Everything is in relationship to the light. See how the leaves in the light are a different color than those in the shadows?"

Turns out you can't look *at* a color to understand it. You have to look *through* it. All colors have a depth. The one color you see is made from shades of others you don't. If you think you see green and get a tube of green, it will look wrong. Flat. One-dimensional. The color we see is never isolated. It is entwined, dependent on others to exist. Life is the same. This moment is connected to others. This pain is connected to past joy, and this joy is connected to future pain. You can't recognize one without the other. My mom paints with heavy brush strokes, and up close each stroke seems isolated and incomplete. But when viewed from a distance under reflected light, the result is an image of life truer than the scene it was painted from.

I've never noticed the color in the shadows, but upon closer observation realize she is right. The clarity of winter's light has given me eyes to see, and the green disappears. I pick new colors. Crimson red. Cadmium yellow. Yellow ocher. Umber. Burnt sienna. Cerulean and cobalt blue. Viridian. Gray. White.

I space the colors evenly around the bottom of my pallet, leaving plenty of room to mix them together. I start with crimson red. As I squeeze the tube, it slowly deposits the color of lifeblood onto the pallet. I then squeeze out the other colors, all rich and slow. I dip the corner of my brush into the cobalt blue and slowly mix it with a little cadmium yellow while adding other colors as my heart leads. It's the color of leaves dancing under glow of the sun. I no longer see green and brown and blue. I see something deeper, more real. Light comes to life and the colors become clear.

The two men who've meant the most to me in this world have been taken. One by force, the other by fate. Yet I am still here. Whether with pain or loss or joy, my heart still beats. My fate is to live. Now I must choose to do so.

With the wisdom of a lifelong artist, Mom stops to remind me, "You can't paint a tree until you learn to see it first."

CHAPTER 23

life insurance

AROUND THE TIME OF MY THIRTY-EIGHTH BIRTHDAY, I decide it may be a good idea to get life insurance because, as you know, thirty-eight is close to forty, and forty is close to—well, let's not talk about it. So I call up my insurance lady to find out how one goes about getting life insurance.

"Do you smoke?"

"No."

"Are you overweight?"

"Define overweight."

She says there will be nothing to worry about. In fact, they will just send someone to our house to do an at-home test and ask a few questions. No big deal. A few days later a young but overweight lady is at my front door reminding me of someone I couldn't quite remember. Maybe it's the scrubs. In her hand is a medical-looking kit with a blood-pressure pump, a needle, and a scale. I find this to be a little medically aggressive for a simple at-home test.

First up is the scale. This doesn't go so well. I try sucking in my gut but it helps about as much as smiling while getting X-rays at the dentist. Then comes the blood-pressure machine. This goes worse. With only these two inputs, the lady in nurse pants concludes I am uninsurable. She uses a couple of medical descriptions to explain my condition. The first is a doctorish way of saying I am fat. The other involves words I don't understand, but plainly translated means that if I don't alter my lifestyle I am headed toward heart failure.

She clearly loves her job, maybe a little too much, and as she goes on with her medical diatribe, it comes to me. She reminds me of that guy who really wants to be a cop but ends up as a mall security guard. Stunned by the prospect of heart failure, I stare off into blank space as she packs her kit and walks back to her car. Just before getting in, she stops and lights a cigarette.

I guess I've always taken my heart for granted, but given this new information that my heart is in imminent danger, I seek out ways to heal it. I'm pretty sure the universal definition of "altering lifestyle" means to diet and exercise, and I figure a good first altering would be more surfing. I love to surf, and surely it could be counted as exercise.

Admittedly, lately my surfing is about as soft as my midsection. I mostly paddle out on sunny days in small waves and bob around catching whatever waves the universe sends my way. Every once in a while I slip off my board and float in my wetsuit, which I like to think of as swimming. After a little of this I let the tide push me to shore, then dry off, put back on my shorts and flip-flops, and go get a coffee and pastry as a reward for having braved the harsh Southern California elements.

After gaining a few more pounds, I take up jogging.

Jogging, also known as running, has always been in the "only when absolutely necessary category" for me, like if you're being chased or if you've eaten too many muffins at the airport Starbucks and are about to miss your flight. I can't imagine doing it on purpose. Some skinny friends of mine are all members of a local gym, so I start my exercise exploration there. The best thing about this gym is that it is mostly full of old people, so there isn't a lot of performance pressure.

Or mirrors. It also has those great treadmills with TVs on them, so while people are jogging they can watch sports or catch up on the news. I mostly watch the food channel. Soon I feel like a hamster on a wheel trying to get the piece of cheese, so I start jogging outdoors.

The best thing about jogging outdoors is that somebody might see you, hopefully from a distance, and think, *Wow, Roger is really getting into shape.* One Sunday morning I'm out trawling for compliments and realize that somehow I am miraculously a couple of miles from home. And there is no way I could get back quick enough to not be late for church. Lately my heart feels like it's hardening toward spiritual things, and I am making an effort to go to church more often.

On Sunday mornings, however, when I'm yelling at my kids to hurry up and put on their shoes, what I really mean is, "Crap, we're late for church again!" And, "Honey, do we really have to go?" And, "If we do have to go, can we at least get a burrito after?" Those last moments before church are like eating a piece of pie before going on a run.

It's not that I don't like church. I just don't like being around people. I also don't like the clap offering. It always feels to me like we are cheering on Jesus as he comes busting out of the tomb and onto the football field. The cheer-angels facing the crowd and leading a competitive chant of "We love Jesus, yes we do. We love Jesus, how 'bout you?!" Behind them, their wings form a tunnel that Jesus will be running through giving low fives. At the end of the tunnel is heaven's high school football coach who will pat Jesus with his clipboard as he comes out and say, "Way to go, number two. You really took one for the team up there."

But by the time our pastor finishes, I feel provoked and challenged and encouraged and am mostly glad to have come. Except now I'm surrounded by people. So as the closing song begins, I plot my escape route, and as I'm safely out the door thinking all's clear, a circle forms. Crap. I'm terrified of those postchurch circles that spontaneously evolve between the front doors and the parking lot. I quickly survey my options.

I could make a one-eighty and head back inside, but that would be like heading into a social meteor field. Too dangerous. I'll have to try to escape the gravitational force, but before I can activate my hyperdrive the Death Star turns on its tractor beam and I'm sucked into the circle. Then as people start talking about their week, it happens.

"Hey, Roger, how are you doing?"

This forces a complex calculation to determine how much they really want to know, so I'm watching to see if they stare off to their car and start listening for stomach growls to evaluate if I need to give a five-second reply or a five-minute accounting. My mind is racing through the weekly issues checklist, organized from emotional turmoil high to low, which makes me think of how I'm losing my job and am terrified of being unemployed, which triggers me to further sort the list from most to least expensive.

"I had to buy a new battery for my car."

The person who started the circle begins talking about how they had to get new tires and we talk about our kids for a while, and then someone else pipes in that they heard the fog is supposed to clear. As I watch their lips moving all I hear is, "Would you like refried or whole beans with that?"

Just as this circle begins to break up and I think I'm free, another one forms a couple of feet away and I make eye contact with someone in it. What is it with these circles? I get sucked into another conversation, and once inside someone asks me how I'm doing. As I begin evaluating my options, my friend Clint steps in. Clint is to me what the blue blanket is to Linus on the Charlie Brown Christmas special. If I could just drape him over my shoulder and carry him everywhere I go, I would do it, because I know it would make me feel safer and more secure. Then someone asks me how my week was. I look over to

Clint, and I know that he knows the neurotic social calculations I'm making. So I confess.

"I think I'm losing my job."

Having said anything at all makes me uncomfortable, but the fact that I just opened a public doorway to one of my fears makes me want to shut it as quickly as possible. Then double bolt it and wrap a chain around it just to be sure it never opens again. I begin thinking of how to retract that information, but before I can come up with rebuttal against myself, Jim says he knows of someone looking for project help and will reach out to him this week. Then Chuck invites me out for a beer. As the others offer different ways they can help, Clint puts his hand on my shoulder, and I feel my heart begin to soften. For a moment everything seems like it will be okay.

To celebrate surviving the circle, I take the family to our favorite local burrito joint. These places are a fixture of the Southern California lifestyle. It's the "other bean" we're all addicted to. As we walk in we're immersed in the comforts of our coastal culture, a vibe complete with surfboards in the rafters, vintage surf art on the walls, and surf videos playing in every corner. The kids love to watch surf videos with their burritos, which I also love, but what I love more is the salsa bar. The modern salsa bar makes a grande decaf two-pump vanilla soy latte out of an otherwise standard burrito.

Standing in front of the salsa bar and debating the various choices and combos available to me, I think more about my life-insurance options. For some reason I have been thinking about Tim a lot lately, and this life-insurance ordeal reminds me of one of our last conversations. He had been researching policies and finally found one he liked and suggested that I should look into it as well. Until that time I hadn't really thought much about it, but as he described the concept it began to sound like a good idea.

Maybe if we purchased it I could actually get on a plane without freaking out. Perhaps, liberated by life insurance, Tim and I would go on that exotic surf trip we always threatened our wives with. Ironically, he only made a single payment before he died. It kind of made me a little happy that he stuck it to the insurance company like that, but it also made me hesitate every time I thought about getting a policy of my own. Afraid of what might happen after the first payment, I'd dropped the idea until now.

I've spent a lot of time being afraid of dying, and as a result some part of me feels like it has already begun the process. It's as though every moment I've spent worrying about mortality is a moment already dead, and the accumulation is a loss of life never to be recovered. Even with issues of less finality, the predator fear preys on the unprotected edges of life, stealing every little bit it can. It's those moments worrying about losing my job or about what will happen if my six-year-old son doesn't get into college, or worrying what the people in the circle will think of me once they realize that I'm worried about what they think of me. Turns out I'm not as afraid of dying as I thought I was. I'm afraid of living.

What kind of insurance is there for that? I need a policy protecting against the gluttony of darkness and its relentless presence along the perimeter. Something to push back the fear when a client calls and says they won't need my services any longer. Something to curb the anxiety that sets in when the doctor says our son needs hearing aids and will never hear the soft rustle of leaves in an autumn breeze. Something to silence the dripping sound of doubt. These are the things robbing my life that no amount of diet or exercise can help.

I can never remember if my wife likes the secret shack sauce or the lime salsa, so I turn around to go ask and looking back to the table see she is talking to some friends from the neighborhood. My wife has been wanting to invite them over for dinner, but I never told her what would be a good night, because, well, I'm busy avoiding people most nights. Knowing that once I get to the table we'll be pulling our calendars from our pockets, I find myself hesitating between the salsas and the soda bar. I realize the lifestyle alteration I need to make isn't making time for exercise. It's making time for people. Which for me may be worse.

Our insurance policy for living isn't with some big insurance company in some big building in some big city far away. When you get the news from the doctor, it won't be an insurance executive coming to your house after the kids are asleep to talk about what you're going to tell them in the morning. Or when you get the call that knocks you to your knees and makes your head spin so badly you can't remember what you had for lunch, or even your own phone number, and you only have the wits about you to find your speed dial.

It will be someone in your circle answering the other line. And they will know in your voice that they need to drop everything and find you. Right now. Then, even if you've never prayed to anyone or anything in your life, words you didn't know will find their way to your lips as you hold together the brokenness until help comes in the form of an angel. In the form of a friend. This is our insurance policy for when life happens.

A couple of months back things started getting bad at work. Then they got worse. I had been in a client-services business, and in a short period lost all my clients. It then seemed that the time I was spending on client work was now spent on worrying about where the next clients would come from. When they didn't come, the worry spiraled into fear. Losing all this business made me feel like a failure, and I didn't want to talk about it, so, without telling me first, my wife mentioned it to some good friends.

Several days later they gave us a gift certificate to a local grocery store. They didn't ask if we needed it, and honestly, if they had I would have said no because my personal pride would have told them that we have plenty of money saved and my spiritual pride would have said that we are trusting God. So they just gave it. Later, cashing the certificate for some milk and bread and food for the kids, I realized that it wasn't about the money. Our friends had infused a little courage into our fear. It was enough to rein in the spiral.

I walk back to the table with one hand on the salsas and one opening my calendar. Over front lawns and fences I talk more to our neighbors that week than I had the entire year prior. Then, at church the following Sunday, as a low-lying fear begins to manifest in my heart, and I'm thinking about making my escape, I am subtly prompted that there is a life-insurance policy that covers this. I find a circle of friends and between the front doors and the parking lot, we talk about our jobs and our kids and how the fog may clear. My heart once again softens with the understanding that it's this circle of people that will keep it from failing.

Regarding the diet and exercise, I'll start next Monday.

CHAPTER 24

secret fishing
hole, part two

MOUNTAINS HOLD THE MYSTERY OF EVERY YOUNG BOY'S imagination. As the boy grows, mountains also hold some of the answers. I return often, looking for clues to the one riddle of my life. I'm always searching. Reading maps and watching stars. Gazing into some distance. Wondering what unknown river runs through it, and if in it I might find the secret fishing hole I've been searching for. I can often sense its presence. As much as I've been searching for it, it has been searching for me. I can feel its breath, like a summer wind warming the back of my neck, whispering promises of discovery.

My oldest son is now old enough to fish, so we're in the mountains on our first fishing trip. A great deal of my parenting has been spent doing all the things with my sons I wished I could have done with my dad. It's a long list of shattered dreams that one by one I'm patching together like a stained-glass window, allowing the sun to once again make them beautiful. My son is seven and has lots of questions. They're endless.

At home, I never seem to have enough time or patience to answer them all, so on this trip I've promised him that if I can, I'll answer every one of them. To prepare, I've been studying Scriptures and stream guides. When he asks about fish I want to be ready. For below every question about fish lies a bigger question about life and God and the meaning of it all. He'll want to know about the fish and the rivers. He'll want to know how God created the mountains and what's on the other side. His entire future view of God will be determined by my answers. I know this, so I prepare for every contingency.

"Daddy?"

"Yes, son."

"How do you catch a fish?"

This is perfect. This is the exact moment I've been waiting for. It's a question that heals a lifetime of hurt, and I'm so thrilled he asked it that I spend a moment to take it all in before answering. I need to get this right. Fatherhood is on the line. So is faith. Images of old Barney flash through my mind. The old man patiently telling me every place a fish might hide and how to attract them to my line. I am ready.

I begin by teaching him how perfectly fish have been created for the world they live. It's as if their bodies have been sculpted by the flow of the river. I then launch into a short lesson of entomology and the life cycle of the various bugs that live on the banks. I explain the difference between a nymph and a dry fly. My mind travels to the Scriptures and the movie *A River Runs Through It*, and I wonder if this is the moment to tell him about how Jesus and the disciples were fishermen, and how fishing can make us more like them.

He is riveted. I can tell his little mind is racing. His moldable, furtive little mind, ready to be filled by the wisdom of his father. He's pausing, winding up for the follow-up question.

"Daddy?"

Here it comes. The big one. He's been waiting to get me alone, to have me to himself. Only then can he ask the question most on his heart. I'm poised and prepared. For the first time as a father, I am equipped for the task that lies ahead. My son pauses, collecting his thoughts, getting the question just right in his head before asking. I am patient. I turn down the radio. I am ready.

"Daddy?"

"Yes, son."

"Who's your favorite Star Wars guy?"

After an incredibly long discussion of Star Wars, we move into another lengthy line of questioning about what my favorite animals are.

"If our doggy wasn't your favorite, what animal would be your favorite?"

I am patient. I am present.

Finally we pull up to the river where my son is reminded of the purpose of this adventure, and as if the last several hours of drawings on the Etch A Sketch are shaken clean, he asks, "Daddy, how do you catch a fish?"

"You have to use the force."

"I knew that."

We are along the Owens River, on the other side of the mountains I fished with my dad. While I was in college my mom told me this area of the Eastern Sierras was his favorite place to go, to think, to fish. He would come here when there was nowhere else. The river meanders through a long, high plains valley, and mountains rise sharply along the edges, towering to more than fourteen thousand feet high on either side. It is the deepest valley in the United States, and looking up from the riverbank, even the biggest problems will seem small in comparison. There are hundreds of rivers and streams cascading from the glaciers and the high mountain meadows of the Sierras.

For a time I thought perhaps the secret fishing hole was on this side of the mountains. Up and down this valley I've driven back roads, where the asphalt turns to dirt, and at the end of the road I've pushed higher up on foot. I've traveled with others and I've traveled alone. I've never found it, but I always sensed it was near.

I am at home along these riverbanks. My soul finds a flow in this river, then rises above, running reckless and wild through fields of summer gold. In the wide-open spaces it expands to fit the vast contours of the valley, creating a basin to accumulate sunrises and sunsets and the heavens between. In this basin, these elements mix with an August rain, creating a substance of concrete in which I find sure footing. Here I am unmoved. I am eternal.

Looking over to my son, I see so much of myself in him. Eyes filled with wonder and heart filled with hope. He's seeing, perhaps for the first time, how big this world is. He wonders what lies beyond the mountains and asks me to take him there. And he's hoping that today, he will catch a fish.

The day is getting late, light low on the horizon, soft and dimensional. We grab our fly rods and gear and walk to the river. The trail is well worn and feels like clouds under our feet.

"Are there river monsters here?"

"Not likely."

"What about bears?"

"I don't think we'll see any bears."

"What about black bears?"

"There aren't any bears here."

"What if we do see bears?"

"Stay next to me. I'll keep you safe."

This section of the Upper Owens River cuts through pasturelands, and we share the moment with a small herd of cows grazing lazily nearby. We come to a section of river that makes an s-curve, enveloping us within its current. My son is eager to cast a line, but there is so much to tell him first. I get down on one knee and pull him close. I want to be at eye level, to emphasize the importance of the wisdom I'm about to pass down from the long line of fathers and sons that have come before. We are all begotten. Part of some bigger whole. I want to teach my son about his place in the stream. I want to teach my son how to read the water.

"Do you see that rock over there, with its top above the water?"

"Yes."

"That is the perfect holding place for a trout."

I explain to my son that in swift waters, trout like to hold behind the safety of a boulder and wait for their food to drift to them in the current. Everything a trout needs is in the flow of the river. The boulder is an easy beginning casting distance away. The air is filled with caddisflies fluttering like abstract thoughts. I grab one to show my son how to pick out a fly to match those hatching around us. I let out enough line from the reel to tie the fly, and as I teach him the science of a clinch knot, I am flooded with memories of being with my dad alongside the riverbank. At the end of this fly line I am retying my broken history.

We have spent hours practicing the art of the fly cast. Before this trip I made a target in our backyard by laying a Hula-Hoop in the grass. Starting from fifteen feet away, we would try to drop the piece of yarn tied to the end of the line into the center of the Hula-Hoop. Like many beginners, my son first wanted to wield the fly rod like a weapon, using the force of his arms to whip the rod back and forth. I tell him to take a deep breath and relax. Casting is not about strength but is about rhythm. In fly-fishing the rhythm is silent. It has to be found, and to find it requires blocking out the noise of the world and stepping into the subtleties of the river. It begins in our minds.

I tell my son to imagine the rod as an extension of his arm. He is connected to it. Likewise, the line is an extension of the rod and the fly to the line. Body, rod, fly line, and fly. It's a single organism. Therefore, when we catch a trout, we are also connected to it. Our deepest longings are for a brief moment entwined in the destiny of a fish, our hearts beating and pulsing to the rhythm of a rainbow trout tugging on the end of our line.

A perfect presentation of a fly begins with the backcast. I stand behind my son in our backyard and gently cradle him, holding his hands in mine. They are so little my hands completely envelop them as I'm showing him how to grip the fly rod. With our right hands we firmly take our grip above the reel and with our left hands hold a little slack in the line. The tip of the rod is pointed toward the target, fifteen feet of line in the grass in front of us, and in a single motion we lift the rod straight out to the height of his chest and we rotate our forearms swiftly back, perfectly perpendicular to the ground, until the rod tip points to a ten o'clock position, slightly behind our heads.

We watch the piece of yarn tied to the end of the line drift over our heads, chasing a tight half-loop in front of it. One count later we feel the line gently pulling the tip of the rod backward, and in the exact opposite motion we rotate our forearms forward toward the Hula-Hoop in the grass and stop the motion at a two o'clock position slightly in front of our heads. The fly line continues chasing the loop until it finally passes it and extends to its furthest reach. It softly floats to the ground in our circle. It's a perfect cast.

We repeat this for a while until my son says that he can feel the rhythm and is ready to try on his own. He doesn't get it at first, but I bring in the target to about ten feet and he is soon consistently landing the fly in the target. Each time he does it he smiles at me, deeply satisfied, and I beam back. Proud. Content. Filled with hope.

As we prepare for my son to cast his first line into the river, my heart is racing.

"Do you remember how we did it in the backyard?"

"Yes."

He lets out a little bit of line.

"Good. Now just let out a little bit more."

"This much?"

"Yes. That's perfect."

He's getting stiff, and I can tell he's a little nervous.

"Everything is okay. Relax. Take a deep breath. You're doing great. Just like we practiced. You've got this."

He loosens up and begins his backcast. I'm watching a film reel of my life. A lonely boy at the edge of the lake. An endless search. A father. A chance to finally chase away the devils that have haunted me my whole life. It's the moment I've looked forward to since the birth of my son.

It's a disaster.

He whips the fly rod back and circles it around his head as if he's trying to lasso the trout. He thinks it's fun, so he does it again and again until the fly line gets tangled in the brush nearby.

"Daddy, look! I caught a bush!"

"That's okay. I'll fix it. Remember, keep the fly rod straight. Remember how we practiced?"

"Yes. I remember."

I get the fly line untangled from the bush and toss it in the water in front of him.

"Remember. Relax. Nice and smooth."

This time he never even brings the rod back over his head. He's slashing the air in front of him like he's sword fighting a bumblebee. He's laughing, thinking this is the most fun ever. It's not fun. It's horrible. Soon the line is tangled like a pile of spaghetti and he gives the rod back to me.

"I don't want to fish anymore."

"What do you mean you don't want to fish? We drove all day to come here and fish. Why don't you sit over there and watch how I fish."

I'm untangling my line and frustrated beyond belief. What kind of a dad can't teach his kid to fish? What kind of a boy doesn't want to fish? What's wrong with him? Do we need to see a counselor? I knew we should have never got him that Wii for Christmas. He's going to end up scaly and white and wondering what those big brown sticks are coming out of the ground with those funny green-shaped things attached to them. I'm trying to solve this parenting dilemma, as tightly wound and screwed up as this fly line.

"Daddy?"

"What."

I'm hoping his brief time out has made him realize that he really does want to fish and that he's ready for more instruction. And that he realizes how awesome I am for bringing him to the mountains and teaching him how to fish in the first place.

"Can I play on your phone?"

"No, you can't play on my phone! You can go play in the dirt."

Then it hits me. This has nothing to do with my son. This has to do with my lifelong search for restoration with my father. I'm using my son, manipulating him to make me whole. I've discovered the depths of my selfishness, realizing just how far I am willing to go to try and heal this pain on my own.

My son is bankside chasing lizards, lost in the freedom of his youth. His innocence, sharp and scalloped as the Eastern Sierra mountain peaks, is like a serrated knife slicing my pain into more manageable pieces. I step into the water and one by one tie them to the end of my line, casting them into the river. There are no fish to rise, but in the search for them I exhaust the remnants of my grief. It drifts mutely in the watercourse, eventually sinking to the bottom of the river where it will collect with the discarded pain of every unknown fisherman, on search for an unnamed fishing hole. These are the secrets of the river. I give myself to it.

This solitude is abruptly ended by the bloodcurdling screams of my little boy. In an instant I am no longer the wounded son but the father, armed and dangerous, ready to rescue. I see my son running toward me at full speed. About twenty yards behind him, also running at full speed, is a half-ton heifer chasing after him. It's a mutant of our insatiable appetite for meat. Bred to grow quickly and be tasty between buns, it runs with the awkwardness of one hundred years of genetic interference.

On multiple levels, I find the scene both worrisome and funny. My son spots me and rather than slowing at the riverbank launches from the edge. I drop everything and catch him midair. He had no doubts that I would. The cow crashes into the water just downstream and ambles its way up the bank on the other side, where it is reunited with the rest of the herd. It wasn't chasing my son. It was chasing its contentment. My perception of what was happening was distorted by my angle.

The sun makes its encore, bowing one last time before the curtain drops. With a river running through high golden plains, with me in the river, with my son in my arms, I see the scars of my life for what they really are. Beautiful sutures, stitching me into the man I've become and the father I will continue to be.

As I am holding my son, a prodigal hope returns and I am made whole. His quivering heart settles against my chest, and as it calms I feel our heartbeats are in sync. We are in rhythm with each other, in rhythm with the moment, in rhythm with the river. We exchange fly rods for stones, and I teach him the art of skipping rocks. He doesn't believe it's possible for a heavy object to skim across the surface but soon he, too, is in on the secret.

I tell him the first one to skip a rock all the way to the other side gets an ice cream, and he begins collecting stones along the riverbank, his smile increasing in size with each one. We don't catch any fish, yet this day is the most perfect day of fishing I've ever had. For after a lifetime of searching, I have finally found my secret fishing hole. Along the water's edge, I am quietly contented when the river gives a closing grace.

"Daddy?"

"Yes, son."

"This is the best day ever."

I watch my son, silhouetted in the flared light of a setting sun. In the distance are mountains beyond mountains.

And heaven beyond that.

———————

The mysteries of the mountains are revealed in the rivers that run through them. All water starts from above. Rain reaches first the mountaintops, then washes over the land, making everything new. It gathers in watersheds, collecting in trickles and streams, returning to the rivers where deep pools reflect the heights from which it came.

Everything flows downhill. Truth. Water. Pain. It collects in the rivers and carves through our thirsty world. We gather at the water's edge. For in the water is truth. And below are trout. As fishermen, we search out these trout because of their proximity to truth. Embedded in the search is a hope that someday we might find what we're looking for.

Time has passed since that fishing trip, and there's a new sadness I can't shake. I cried a lot as a child, looking from the front window of a house at the edge of the Sumps, at a driveway empty except for the oil stains of an old, faded-blue truck that was never coming home. I've begged most of my life for God to take away this pain. I've missed my father at every stage of life, but it wasn't until that fishing trip with my son that I realized how much he missed me too.

Every father gets a hope for his son. Mine wanted to be a better dad. He wanted to be free from his addictions. He wanted to watch me grow into a man. He missed so much of my life. All of it. He wanted to take me to the secret fishing hole even more than I wanted to go. I've been told there are no tears in heaven. I think it's a lie.

I never found the secret fishing hole because I didn't recognize the trail. Now that I've been, I wondered if there was another that led to the place Dad first described in our tiny apartment kitchen. Not long ago I was sitting in my office staring blankly at an even blanker computer screen. I had a cold and was shrouded in the haze of cold syrup and cough drops, desperately seeking a word, something to put on a page. Something to redeem an already gloomy day. Nothing would come.

Still I stared and begged for God to reveal something true. My heart began to wander, and moments turned to hours. It ascended into clarity and could see farther than before. In the distance was something beautiful. This had never happened before and hasn't happened since. If it weren't for a sense left behind in my soul, I would be tempted to think it never really did happen.

Through my heart I saw a dense light descending on a meadow illuminated in infinite colors of gold. Winding through the wildflowers was an unnamed river. Along a curve in its bank was a tree in full bloom. The air thick with life. As I got closer to the tree I could see a figure of a man I didn't recognize. Suddenly my eyes filled with tears, and through this watery magnifying glass I could see deeply into my soul.

It was my dad, standing alone in the shade of the tree. He was himself, but more so. No bruises or scars. The bags under his eyes replaced with lines caused from a lifetime of laughter. He was perfect. His eyes drew me nearer, and when he smiled, I was a child again,

CHAPTER 25

first day of summer

I WAS RECENTLY BUILDING A PIECE OF FURNITURE AND RAN down to the hardware store to pick up some supplies when I heard my name called from behind.

"Hey, Roger!"

A guy in his early thirties was walking toward me with a smile I remembered but couldn't place.

"It's me, Derrick. I used to work for you and Tim at Skate Street."

It all came back.

"Wow. How are you?"

"I'm doing good. Really good in fact."

In memory Derrick is fixed as a kid, and I have to adjust to the young man standing in front of me. I thought for sure I'd never forget the people or the faces or the thousands of stories of Skate Street. The tragedy of time is how a beautiful dream can hold our hearts hostage for a month or a day or a decade, taking them over completely, and one day disappear behind a mist of lapsed memory, as if it had never come at all. Alongside Tim, I gave some of the best years of my life to this dream. When he died it was a double funeral. Behind our grief the world goes on, our suffering as unnoticed as our toil. All vanities. A chasing of the wind.

Derrick said he had been working at the hardware store for a while and had really gotten his life together. He was sober. He was going to church. He knew I would be pleased to hear this, and I was. He then paused for a moment and said there was something he really wanted to tell me.

He said after Tim fired him for stealing from us, he continued to check in on him. I tried to recall Tim telling me that. If he did, I'd forgotten and was encouraged to hear it. Derrick said Tim never abandoned him, no matter how bad his choices. There was so much more, he said, that he wished he could have told Tim. I told him I felt the same. He shook my hand and apologized for stealing from us. I thanked him and told him how great it was to see him, then turned to pay for my supplies.

"Hey, Roger, one more thing."

His smile was gone, face full of sincerity.

"Working for you and Tim was the best thing that ever happened to me. I just thought you should know that."

It's been seven years since Tim died. In every major religion, seven is a sacred number. In my own, it represents perfection. Completion. It was through seven cows by the river that Pharaoh first learned of God. He had a dream, a vision of seven fattened cattle followed by seven lean ones.

Searching for the meaning, he was failed by the magicians and the wise men of the age. When nothing of his world could satisfy, he sent for a man from another. He pulled Joseph from prison, and after Joseph told Pharaoh the meaning of the dream—that seven years of plenty were coming, followed by seven years of famine—Joseph was restored to power and influence. Through the plenty he ruled over the land, second only to Pharaoh. But in this excess he was not fully restored.

When the land went barren, Joseph's brothers traveled from their homeland to seek blessing from the one who could keep their family from starvation, not knowing it was the brother they had sold into slavery. When they found him, Joseph had everything the world could offer: riches beyond measure, power and influence, even the opportunity to exact revenge upon the brothers who meant him harm. Instead, he extended grace. He then asked for the one thing that could make him whole. To be reunited with his father. Joseph was restored through the famine.

In my life, time has not healed. Wounds run deep and scars remain. Not a day goes by that I don't think of my dad and Tim and the things we did and the things we should have done. I miss them. It still hurts. I suppose it always will. In the adolescence of my pain I fought it blindly, clumsily as a foal's first steps. Somehow suffering matures, and seven years later I've stopped asking for the pain to disappear. Instead, I am asking for it to be made complete.

Like all created things, pain has a life cycle. It lives. It dies. And it lives again in a different form. As if it has a purpose. In time pain can be redeemed, ground down to its purest substance, as perfect as the pure quartz of a white-sand beach. Redeemed pain is the beauty mark of a fallen world. I'm ready to leave the seven years of famine, bringing with me only the pain that has been completed. And through it I will see the world afresh. And I will love. Until I am made complete with it.

I just turned forty, and nothing has turned out the way I planned. I thought by now I'd know more of what I wanted in life. That I'd be more financially secure. That there'd be fewer doubts. I sit in a borrowed office, at a borrowed desk, in a borrowed chair, with windows that look across the street to the junior high where I first met Tim, and I feel like I haven't made it very far in life.

In the morning I watch as kids walk to school, circling by my window from left to right, like fish in an aquarium. Most swim giddily, flurrying between friends to protect from the dangers of the reef while chattering incessantly about boys and scary movies, bright colors of clothing all identifying marks that they belong together. Others swim alone. Faces lifeless, shoulders hunched under the invisible weight of life's broken promises. They seem so young to be carrying so much, but I know from my own experience how heavy life can be at that age.

A young boy stops in front of my office window. I wave, but he just stares as if I don't exist. Or I exist in some lesser form. Suddenly I'm the one in the aquarium, swimming through my office in a rolling chair, stacking and restacking my output. As he stares through a reflection of an older self, I want to tell him that everything will be okay. To grab the frayed end of hope and let it drag him through the turbulence into the deep. That there he will find his freedom. Instead I stare mutely, silent as his pain.

In many ways I'm back to where I started. At the edge of the same playground where the long arm of a young boy with poofy white shirtsleeves pulled me out of one life and into another. But, through the journey, the place is now new. I've been through the plenty. I've been through the famine. Through lenses of loss and love I can now see farther. Beyond this boy in front of me. Beyond the boy behind me. To secret places, lost for a time, now rediscovered.

———

Spring comes early to this section of coast. While the rest of the country slumbers through long winter's nights, mustard grass blossoms along coastal hills, cascading like yellow waterfalls into Pacific blue. In younger years I would rise early to meet the day surfing the base of these wildflower waterfalls. Then I believed spring would bloom eternal. After the dark winter of my childhood, I even believed I deserved it.

I have since learned that all colors fade. For along these coasts, after spring comes the fog, blotting the sun, sodden as a wet woolen blanket. For far too long life has lumbered through remnants of night, each day fading deeper into the absence of light. In days of gray I've cursed the sun for teasing me with a summer that never came. In fog, there are no shadows to point north.

Time passes. South swells turn to north swells, then back to south. Joy turns to pain turns to joy. I'm now teaching my sons to surf, and these shores of my youth are filled with more angels than ghosts. For after a lifetime of searching, I now know I can be the father I've been searching for. After mending the loss of a friend, I can be the friend who mends the loss for others. I can sell out the Ventura Theater. I can live a life that matters. I've realized, though, this life is mine to give, it's not mine to own. In these holy waters I am transformed.

The ocean surges and as I turn to my boys my heart swells with resolve. I will give my life to them. I will teach them the secrets of the journey: how to recognize joy and embrace it at every turn—how to expect pain but not fear it—how to believe that beyond the pain there is a hope, and in it, the fingerprints of God. I will teach them to love. That the fullest hearts are those that have given the most. That they have loved and have lost, have been broken and mended, and broken and mended again. I will prepare them for their own journies. And pray they find their own way home.

In morning fog the day is filled with promise, and I stand knee deep in the Pacific, looking over an endless horizon and the boundless gifts of the ocean. I paddle out, and as I'm met by the waves, dive under. I'm dunked and lifted. I've found my peace in the water.

The first wave arrives and I am met by God. I reach into the deep with hands cupped and yearning. Aging arms stretched to their limits, reaching forward and pulling back over and over, and the force of current gives me power. To paddle, to stand, to walk on water. I am in the curl of the wave, arms stretched wide, embracing the life that's been given: the grief, the sorrow, the regrets, the fears, the doubts, the shame. The joy. On the rising tide of a late-spring swell, I am in the untrespassed flow of water, being made new.

The surf session ends, and as I rise from the ocean my face is met with the sun, breaking through the gray and the gloom, opening windows to brightened blue. The fog is lifting. It feels like the first day of summer.

Afterword

THIS STORY IS STILL VERY MUCH ALIVE. AFTER COMPLETING the manuscript, I went to breakfast with Tim's mom, dad, and sister to get their thoughts on the book and make sure events were portrayed accurately. We've remained close over the years and I've been inspired by how they've directed their grief. Tim's dad now works with guys struggling with alcohol abuse and Tim's mother and sister volunteer with a group called Compassionate Friends, supporting families after the death of a child.

At the end of breakfast, Tim's mom and I were walking to our cars when she stopped and delivered a challenge. After saying she'd use this story to help those she walks alongside after losing a family member, she turned and asked what I planned to do for someone who identifies with the challenges of this book.

Life is hard. We all know people who are struggling with loss. Or grief. Or addiction. Or loneliness. Or we struggle with these things ourselves. Maybe we struggle with wounds inflicted by our fathers. Or maybe we want to be better fathers. Or maybe we are trying to discover our best selves—ones that would sell out the Ventura Theater.

Whatever it is keeping you up at night, my hope for you, your family, or your friends walking through the challenges of this life, is that you have someone walking with you. If not, please consider going to www.mybestfriendsfuneral.com. I've talked with a number of people and organizations who would love to walk with you. Their contact information is located on the website. I also have some recommendations for further resources and books that have been meaningful to me. I even know some fly-fishing guides who can help you find a secret fishing hole.

Life is also beautiful. And made more so as we do it together.

Acknowledgments

I'd like to first acknowledge those who made this book possible: My good friend Alex Field, who first listened to the eulogy at the Ventura Theater and has encouraged me to write about it ever since. My writing mentor, Pamela K. Long Brackley, who helped me realize I was writing about something bigger. And my spiritual mentor, Don Loomer, who encouraged me through every doubt.

I'd like to acknowledge the folks at Thomas Nelson who believed in this story and helped bring it to life. Thank you, Brian Hampton, for bringing me into the Thomas Nelson family. Thank you, Kristen Parrish, Janene MacIvor, and Jen McNeil for making me sound much better than I deserve. And thanks to Chad Cannon, Kimberly Boyer, and Tiffany Sawyer for making sure this effort doesn't just end up as a pile of books in my garage.

Next I'd like to acknowledge Tim's family who were so helpful and supportive through the entire writing process. Miki and Gavin, your strength and grace inspire me. Tim's dad Frank, mom Lynne, and sister Paula, thank you for letting me share your stories and for being a part of mine.

ACKNOWLEDGMENTS

Though it would be impossible to list them all here, I'd like to acknowledge a few friends for their roles in this effort. Clint Garman, for being a part of this story from the beginning, and for still being a part of it now. Braden and DeNai Jones, for their constant inspiration and support. Greg and Katie Bayless, whose commitment from the first word and unwavering belief in me has given me courage to do this. Phil and Cari Stone, for the countless hours listening to every potential idea for this book (and then for reading them again later). And Erik Payne, for filling in the gaps of my memory based on a long history of friendship.

I'd like to also extend a special thanks to Greg Russinger for walking through some of the hardest parts of this story with me; Tracy, Dave, and the staff at Rabalais for providing a place to write this story; and to Karley Mase and Dennis Shelton who helped me figure out how to share the story with those who might need it. And to coconspirators Jeff Lilley, Steve McBeth, David Kinnaman, Bryan Jennings, and Michael Blanton for their commitment to me in every effort, book or otherwise.

I'd like to also thank my family: Grandma Thompson, who has convinced me that not only am I perhaps the greatest writer in the world, but I'm likely the most handsome. (I promise, Grandma, I'll be careful!) Thanks to Grandpa (and Grandma) Davis for teaching me how to use a table saw and what side of the sidewalk to walk on when you are with a woman and all the other things that help one become a man. Thanks to Grandma Nantha who loved me from afar. To my mom, the list of things to thank you for could be the subject for another book. A big one. Instead, I'll just say that I love you. And a huge thanks goes to my sister, Rachel Plasch, for our "Tuesdays with Roger" sessions and for pushing me to be the best writer (and person) I can be. A good deal of this story is as much yours as it is mine.

ACKNOWLEDGMENTS

Lastly I want to thank my boys. Hayden and Austin, I could not be more proud of who you are becoming. And Melissa, my one true love, who continues to make me want to be the man she deserves. Any accomplishment of mine is equally yours.

I'd like to make a special acknowledgment here. Grandpa Thompson passed away before the book was published. A few days before he passed, I was able to read him the manuscript. We cried and laughed through the reading and at the end he whispered thinly to me, "Beautiful, Rog. Just beautiful." I will always feel the same about him.

About the Author

ROGER PRODUCES SURF MOVIES WITH WALKING ON WATER Films and works with orphans in Haiti with the Hands and Feet Project.

Roger and Tim (the best friend in this book) began in the surf and skate industry with a small surf clothing company and surf shop. They then opened the world-renowned skate park, Skate Street Ventura. Since then, Roger has designed skate parks, retail stores, youth camps, and entertainment venues throughout the country. He has produced surf and skate movies and has collaborated in the entertainment, fashion, and publishing industries. In addition, Roger has served on numerous nonprofit and ministry boards.

When not working, Roger can be found fly-fishing, building furniture, and surfing with his sons near the coastal town of Ventura, California, where he lives with his wife, two young sons, one old dog, and seven productive chickens.

- For more information on the work in Haiti, or to get involved, visit: HandsAndFeetProject.org.

- For more information on surf camps and films, visit: WalkingOnWater.com.
- If you'd like to contact Roger, or have him collaborate on any of your projects, you can reach him at: heyrog@rogerwthompson.com.

WALKING ON WATER

DEDICATED TO SHARING THE GOSPEL OF JESUS CHRIST WITH THE GLOBAL SURFING COMMUNITY SINCE 1995

SURF CAMPS

FILMS

OUTREACH EVENTS

MISSION TRIPS

WWW.WALKINGONWATER.COM

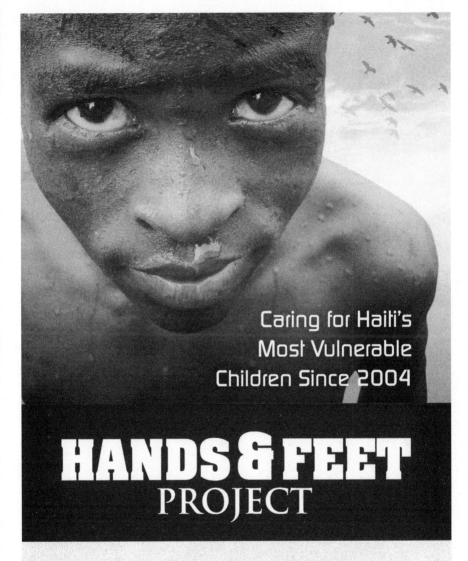

Caring for Haiti's
Most Vulnerable
Children Since 2004

HANDS & FEET
PROJECT

Children's Villages in southern Haiti providing
family-style care, child sponsorships,
and mission trip hosting.
To learn more visit **HandsandFeetProject.org**